WORLD RELIGIONS

THE ESSENTIAL REFERENCE GUIDE TO THE WORLD'S MAJOR FAITHS

Author: Debbie Gill

With: Ras Kwende B. Anbessa-Ebanks, Stephen Batchelor,
Shahin Bekhradnia, Dr Brian Bocking, Alan Brown,
Jonathan Gorsky, Umar Hegedüs, Sister Victoria Hummell,
Dilip Kadodwala, Dr Vinod Kapashi, The Hon. Barney Leith,
Indarjit Singh and Dr Yao

First published in 1997 by
Collins, an imprint of
HarperCollins Publishers
77-85 Fulham Palace Road
Hammersmith
London W6 8JB

This new edition first published in 2003

The Collins website address is www.collins.co.uk

Collins is a registered trademark of HarperCollins Publishers Ltd

09 08 07 06
7 6 5 4

This book was conceived, designed and produced by Flame Tree Publishing, part of The Foundry
Creative Media Company Limited, Crabtree Hall, Crabtree Lane, London SW6 6TY

General consultant of the main edition: Elizabeth Breuilly
Overall authenticator of the main edition: Robert Vint
Special thanks to Vicky Garrard and Chris Herbert

A catalogue record for this book is available from the British Library

ISBN-13 978 0 00 715893 5
ISBN-10 0 00 715893 9

Printed and bound by Printing Express Ltd, Hong Kong

Contents

Introduction

A s far back as we can discover, people have asked questions that still trouble us today, both practical questions about how to live, how to treat other people, how to avoid unhappiness, and transcendental questions such as What is the meaning of life? How did the universe come into being? Why does suffering exist? What happens after death?

Religion in its many different forms sets out to answer these and other questions.

For much of the 20th century, religion has been regarded by many in the West as irrational and irrelevant or, alternatively, too sensitive a subject for discussion. In recent years, however, there has been a huge upsurge of interest in religion, among students, seekers and believers. For most of human history, religion has given shape and meaning to most people's lives. If it has not been discussed, this was only because it was so well understood and universally accepted within any one society. When faith meets faith, or when faith meets unbelief, both in today's 'global village', and in the past with the slower movement of people, there are arguments, often violence and heartache, but also challenge, change and discovery.

Many people feel that the more we know about each other's beliefs, the easier it will be to avert persecution of one faith or belief system by another. But knowledge alone is not sufficient. All too often knowledge about a faith has been used as the basis of ridicule or distortion, or of more focused and informed insult. What is needed is not just knowledge, but understanding. While a book like this can inform, it is almost impossible for a general book to convey what a faith means to its adherents, and how that faith shapes the unfolding of their lives. What it can do is give enough background to begin a meaningful discussion with someone of another faith, or to go deeper into items in the news. There will be statements that you disagree with, possibly even in relation to your own faith, and ideas you find strange, but treat that as a starting point.

Elizabeth Breuilly, ICOREC

Nepalese figure of a Bodhisattva – or 'Buddha-in-waiting' – a saviour and helper of the needy.

≈ EARLY RELIGIONS ≈

Egypt

The great pyramids in Egypt, which predate the birth of Christ by 3000 years, were built as the last resting-places of the Pharaohs.

The highly organized, centrally-administered civilization of ancient Egypt was something new in the world. For more than 3000 years it offered a way of life which centred on towns, and had a rigid class structure.

The development of writing was of great significance to the Egyptian culture, and has allowed future generations to understand a great deal about this complex and important civilization.

Sacrifice and ritual held central positions in religious life, and the priesthood was a powerful class. Over the years, changes took place in the religious world and affected the Egyptians' customs. The complex array of gods evolved and coalesced; half-human and half-animal, they represented the mighty natural forces which were part of everyday life in Egypt, for the prosperity of the empire rested on the Nile, which flooded its banks annually, bringing down fertile silt in which to sow the crops. In turn, these were ripened by the daily sunshine.

The Egyptian tomb paintings and death masks found in the pyramids are of unsurpassed beauty and skill, especially the glorious, golden mask of the young Pharaoh Tutankhamen.

The Egyptians used no sacred books, nor a revelation of divine truth. Myths and legends told the stories of the gods and their relationships with one

Golden death mask of the pharaoh Tutankhamen. ▶

another, and reinforced the sacred hierarchy. A belief in the afterlife was at the heart of the religion. Bodies were prepared for the grave as if for a journey to the afterworld, mummified and accompanied by treasure for the voyage. Even animals were prepared in this way, particularly those which were considered sacred, such as cats.

The Egyptian *Book of the Dead* was designed to be given to the dead on their entombment. This was a book of instructions on how to manage death and the afterlife.

Anubis, the god of death, was one of the complex array of Egyptian gods which evolved during this ancient civilization.

South America

The ancient cultures of Middle and South America are known to us only from archaeology and from the accounts of the Spanish conquistadors who destroyed them in the 16th century. Their leadership structure seems to have been partly expressed religiously, with government and religion closely interwoven into a highly organized whole.

The Maya and Aztec peoples produced a wealth of statues and gold and silver artefacts depicting the gods in their various guises, from Xipe Tolec, shown clad in the flayed skin of a sacrificial victim, to Quetzalcoatl, the Feathered Snake.

The religion of the Olmecs, who lived between about 1200 and 500 BCE in what is now Mexico, centred on the sacred jaguar, who seems sometimes to have combined with other animals or birds to form new deities.

Mayan deities, who were believed to require offerings in the form of human sacrifices.

9

Successors to the Olmecs were the Maya, whose state religion was based on ceremonial centres dominated by imposing pyramidal temples.

Mayan gods, also frequently a combination of animals and birds, were deemed to require regular offerings, which frequently took the form of human sacrifice.

The Aztecs, a martial race living in Central America from about the 12th century CE until the Spanish conquest in 1532, worshipped the sun and sacrificed to it a constant stream of human victims. Perhaps as many as 20,000 prisoners of war were slain each year.

The Inca civilization of Peru existed at roughly the same time as that of the Aztecs. Their religion, founded on ritual, divination and sacrifice, was not so much spiritual as practical, with the cohesion it offered providing the framework for an efficient network for the supply of food to a widely spaced population.

Many other South American peoples, the Chavin, Moche and Chimu among them, worshipped moon deities or feline cults. If they had not already died out by the time of the Spanish conquest, the forceable imposition of Roman Catholicism saw an end to all the folk religions of South and Middle America.

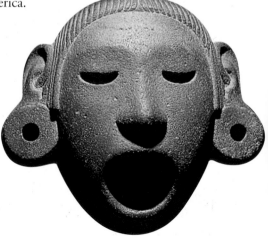

Mask of the Aztec god Xipe Tolec.

Greece and Rome

The ancient Greeks lived in a world inhabited by gods who were depicted in human terms, but were immortal. Communication with them was frequent, by means of prayer, divination, omens and sacrifice. The gods often spoke to humans through the medium of an oracle or soothsayer. Special temples were built for these oracles, most famously the one at Delphi.

The Parthenon in Athens, Greece, is a temple to the goddess Athena and is also one of the world's finest examples of Doric architecture.

The Parthenon in Athens.

The religion of the ancient Romans was a complex mixture, centred on family cults, with the worship of ancestors and household gods often concerned with agriculture and reproduction. When their burgeoning empire absorbed that of Greece, they accepted also the Greek gods, adapting them to suit their own culture and beliefs. The Roman cult of Mithras arose around CE 90. The main theme of the cult was the slaying of a bull, and in the many Mithraic sites which have been excavated can be found depictions of this event, with other motifs capable of astrological interpretation – perhaps a star chart for the soul's journey to salvation.

The army provided most recruits to the Mithraic religion, and temples are to be found from Hadrian's Wall to Alexandria in Egypt.

Hadrian's Wall, where the ruins of a Mithraic temple can be found.

Old European

The Celtic figure of a god with horns or antlers is a frequently-found symbol of fertility. The severed human head is another widespread feature of Celtic imagery, and it is believed that sacrifice, including human sacrifice, took place at wells and streams.

Christianity was slow to penetrate Northern Europe; the Celtic and the Germanic peoples, related in race and the structure of their religions, clung to their old ways. Everything we know of their religions comes from a few scanty sources: early Roman writers; archaeological finds. The fragments must be pieced together to form fragile generalizations.

From the prevalence of carefully prepared and furnished graves it would appear that the Celts believed in the afterlife. The Other World was always close by, with points of access at many sacred places – later to be appropriated by Christians as sites for their churches.

The Druids were mentioned by several classical writers, but the nature of their learning and influence remains uncertain. They appear to have been priests and arbitrators, playing a major role in ceremony and divination, in healing and astronomy.

The Roman writer Tacitus admired the Teutons for their military prowess, their vigour and simplicity. They were a polytheistic people, and their gods were often described by contemporary Roman writers as identifying with their Roman equivalents.

We know more about the Norse gods, mainly because of the work of saga tellers such as Snorri Sturluson of Iceland (who died in CE 1264). There were two groups of gods: first was the Aesir, or great gods, who lived in Asgard and were proactive gods. The second group was the Vanir, or lesser gods, the

Painting showing the Ride of the Valkyries who were war maidens for the Norse god Odin.

reactive gods. The great ruler of the afterworld was Odin, whose war maidens, the Valkyries, chose warriors for Valhalla, the great hall in the sky where days were spent in battle and nights in feasting. The great thunder god, Thor, and Loki, the enigmatic trickster figure, were also members of the Aesir. Frey, the god of fertility, was of the Vanir. However, even the gods were not immortal: it was believed that with the great storm of Ragnarök would come the end of the world, vividly described as the twilight of the gods, or Götterdämmerung.

- Tuesday – Tiwas's day
- Wednesday – Wodan's day
- Thursday – Thor's day
- Friday – Frey's day

Celtic stone figure found in a pagan shrine in Ireland.

THE
⤳ BAHÁ'Í FAITH ⤳

- Originated in Persia, CE 1844.
- Holy Book – the *Kitab-i-Aqdas,* by Bahá'u'lláh.
- Approximately 7 million followers worldwide.

The Bahá'í Faith, a new religion which emerged from the Shi'ite branch of Islam, sees itself as the latest but not the last appearance of 'the ancient faith of God'. It is claimed to be one of the great universal religions of the world, with a community numbering between 6 and 7 million people in more than 200 countries. In terms of geography, it comes second only to Christianity as the most widespread religion.

Tomb of the Báb, the forerunner of Bahá'u'lláh who was the founder of the Bahá'í Faith.

The Origins of the Bahá'í Faith

The Lives of the Founders

In 1844, a young Persian visionary named Siyyid 'Alí-Muhammad took the title 'the Báb', meaning 'the Gate', and announced the imminent appearance of a messenger from God, who would be the most recent of a long line which included Moses, Zoroaster, Buddha, Jesus Christ and Muhammad.

The Báb was persecuted by dominant Muslim leaders of the time and eventually executed for his teachings, but his message had spread widely. His followers, too, were massacred or exiled.

Mírzá Hussayn-'Alí was one of those followers to be imprisoned and tortured. During four months chained in the notorious 'Black Pit' dungeon in Tehran, he experienced a revelation that he was the prophet foretold by the Báb. Exiled to Baghdad, he announced his mission in CE 1863. His followers knew him as Bahá'u'lláh, the 'Glory of God'.

From Baghdad, Bahá'u'lláh was summoned to Constantinople. He was then further exiled to Adrianople and, in 1868, to Acre, where he wrote a series of letters to world rulers, exhorting them to reconcile their differences and instead devote their energies to establishing world peace. While under house arrest in Acre, Bahá'u'lláh revealed the key work of his faith, the *Kitab-i-Aqdas*, 'The Most Holy Book'. He remained (officially) a prisoner until his death in 1892, although he was allowed to live outside Acre during the last years of his life.

The Message

- God as a transcendent being.
- The essential unity of religion.
- The unity in diversity of humankind.

The central message of the Bahá'í Faith is one of unity and the breaking down of traditional barriers of race, class and creed. God, transcendent and unknowable but manifest in his creation, has provided successive revelations to mankind via a series of Divine Messengers whose common purpose has been to bring humankind to spiritual maturity. Each of these messengers has been the founder of one of the world's great religions.

According to the United Nations, the Bahá'í international community works in partnership with others for universal peace and is strongly against all forms of prejudice, persecution and conflict. The purpose of life is seen as coming to know and worship God, and the development of God-given capacities, both to enhance one's own life and for the service of humanity.

Bahá'ís on pilgrimage entering the Shrine of the Báb to pray.

Worship

There is no priesthood or set form of worship. Each local community meets once every nineteen days for the Nineteen Day Feast, with its three-part programme of worship, community consultation and socializing. Worship includes prayers and readings from the scriptures of the Bahá'í Faith and of other religions.

A Bahá'í house of worship.

- The Bahá'í Faith houses of worship are open to all.
- Each house of worship has nine sides and a central dome, symbolizing both the diversity and the unity of the human race.
- Decorative motifs include symbols of the various world faiths.

The Structure of the Bahá'í Faith

The Bahá'í world spiritual and administrative centre of the Bahá'í Faith is at Haifa in the Holy Land. The Universal House of Justice, the elected governing body of the Bahá'í world, directs spiritual and administrative matters. In countries, cities and villages throughout the world, national and local elected assemblies deal with all matters relating to the community, including education.

The Seat of the Universal House of Justice on Mount Carmel.

The Spread of the Bahá'í Faith

B etween 1911 and 1913 Bahá'u'lláh's eldest son, Abbás Effendi, usually known as 'Abdu'l-Bahá, travelled throughout Europe and America taking his father's teachings to the people of the West. Since then the faith has spread throughout the world, with the largest group in India. Even today, however, the Bahá'ís in Iran are still suffering persecution.

'Abdu'l-Bahá, the eldest son of Bahá'u'lláh.

BUDDHISM

- Gautama Buddha, born around 586 BCE in what is now Nepal.
- 'Buddha' means 'Enlightened One'.
- Approximately 330 million Buddhists worldwide.

Buddhism is a practice aimed at liberating the human mind from anguish. Its three vital elements are: first, the narrative of the life of Buddha; second, the philosophical world-view he put forward; and third, the institution of Buddhism (that is, Buddha's followers).

Gautama Buddha, the legend of whose life forms the basis of the Buddhist religion.

The Origins of Buddhism

The Life of the Buddha

There is little historical detail surrounding the life of Siddharta Gautama, believed to be the latest and most holy of a long line of buddhas, but it is the legend of his life which is the core of the Buddhist religion. The Buddha was born around 586 BCE to a princely family of the warrior caste, a family which sheltered him from the hardships of ordinary life. However, while out of the palace one day he saw three things: an invalid, an old man, and a corpse. (Some texts state that the Buddha also saw a fourth sight: a holy man who had renounced all the pleasures of life.) The shock of these sights forced him to rethink his values and his lifestyle and, although Gautama now had a wife and a baby son, he left his family to search for truth and knowledge, and for a way to free mankind from the pain of fear and suffering. This was the beginning of Gautama's nomadic life of reflection, study and austerity.

Bronze and gold statue depicting the Buddha's revelation under the bodhi tree.

He finally achieved the revelation he sought: at a place called Bodh-Gaya, during meditation under a sacred peepul tree (or *bodhi* tree, often called 'bo tree'), he received a full insight into the nature of the world.

As Gautama had now attained enlightenment, he was henceforth known by the honorific title 'the Buddha'. Buddha means 'Enlightened One', and denotes a state of being, the state of the direct awareness of *dharma*. Thereafter, he travelled round India, teaching and winning disciples. He died when about 80 years old – his death having been foretold by heavenly portents.

The Appeal of Buddhism

Buddhism arose at a time when religious revival and renewal was sweeping the world. It grew out of the Hindu religion, a tradition which had long been in existence. Buddhism shared some central ideas with Hinduism, especially that of reincarnation, and the law of cause and effect – *karma*. However, Buddha did make a decisive break with Hinduism, in that his teachings did not centre upon belief in gods (although he did not deny the existence of God or gods). He also rejected the caste system, and sacrificial cults.

The Teachings

Buddhists' aims:

- To seek *dharma* (an untranslatable word, loosely meaning 'insight').
- To achieve *nirvana* (a state of relief from the pain and anxiety of the world).
- To reach freedom from *karma* (the endless cycle of rebirth).

B uddhism is not centred upon veneration of any kind: Buddha is not a god, nor a heavenly mediator, nor a redeemer, and the most important thing for a disciple of his to seek is direct recognition of *dharma*. Enlightenment and salvation are linked – Buddha's knowledge, so painfully gained, was not simply intellectual knowledge, but an insight. His central insight concerned the interdependence and impermanence of all things.

The main aim of Buddhism is to realize *nirvana*: the true refuge, the eternal realm, liberation from *karma* and freedom from all ties to this world and its cycle of rebirth. The ineffable state of *nirvana* can only be achieved by meditation, austere practices and great personal effort. Study and instruction are only capable of pointing a student in the right direction.

Buddhists achieve nirvana through meditation and austere practices.

The Buddha taught that, although humans do have free will, the law of *karma* operates in all dimensions of human life. *Karma* is the force created by evil deeds or bad feelings, which binds people to the cycle of death and rebirth. Through reincarnation, humans suffer the consequences, good or bad, of their previous lives. It is this legacy which leads to *dukkha,* or suffering, in their present lives. However, it is possible to transcend the effects of *karma* by resisting desires until, like an untended fire, *karma* dies down.

Buddhists strive to reach freedom from the endless cycle of death and rebirth (karma).

Sacred Texts

B uddhist texts produced in India in the 11th and 12th centuries CE were written on palm leaves and strung with cord to produce books. They were often philosophical treatises on the nature of wisdom and compassion, and were beautifully illustrated with scenes from the life of Buddha, in bright colours, featuring especially brilliant red and yellow.

The Buddhist faith has a huge range of sacred texts of which one example is the *Pali Canon*. Written originally in Pali, an ancient North Indian language, it contains the teachings and sermons of Buddha; it is divided into three sections known as *pitaka* ('baskets'). This book is not known by all Buddhists as each school of Buddhism has its own canon.

Pali scriptures.

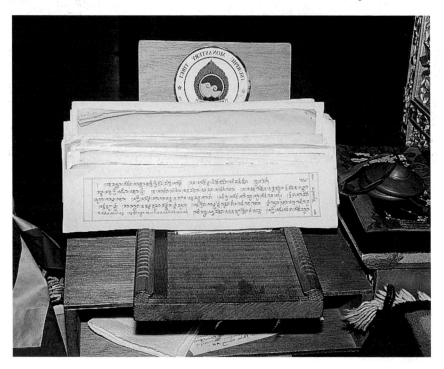

The Practices of Buddhism

Buddhism is moderate in all ways, and the desired result is complete insight and serenity. A central conviction of the faith is that one should cause no harm to others, and for this reason Buddhists are often vegetarian.

A Buddhist monk is said to need only three robes. These are saffron in colour and include a *dhoti* (a long cloth wrapped round the waist) and a shawl round the shoulders.

Buddhist saffron robes, including a dhoti and a shawl.

The Buddhist attempts to free his mind from delusion, and to attain a state of enlightenment by exercises of concentration and meditation. Buddhist monks and nuns are sometimes hermits and sometimes live communally.

There are certain ways by which a Buddhist can gain merit: one way is to give alms; another is by visiting the important sites of Buddha's life. In the early years of the religion, Buddhist remains were installed in cairns, precursors of the great *stupas* of classical Buddhist temples.

Buddhist Philosophy

Ethical conduct is defined by the **Five Precepts,** or guidelines:

1 Take no life.

2 Do not steal – be generous.

3 Abstain from sexual misconduct.

4 Abstain from wrong speech – do not tell lies.

5 Abstain from intoxicants.

The core of the Buddha's philosophy is to follow the **Four Noble Truths**:

1 All life is permeated by suffering or non-satisfaction *(dukkha),* the effect of *karma.*

2 The cause of suffering is craving *(tanha)* and a misplaced sense of values.

3 Craving, and therefore suffering, can be eliminated. Freedom from recurring delusion, or *samsara,* leads to *nirvana.*

4 The way to enlightenment is by following the **Noble Eightfold Path**.

THE NOBLE EIGHTFOLD PATH

- Right understanding
- Right speech
- Right occupation or livelihood
- Right awareness

- Right attitude
- Right action
- Right effort
- Right composure

The Noble Eightfold Path is known also as the 'Middle Way', because it is balanced and practical, not extremist. It can be divided into three aspects: truth and insight; ethical conduct; and spiritual discipline.

The Spread of Buddhism

Buddhism in India

After the death of Gautama, Buddhism flourished, spreading to Central and South-East Asia, Japan, China and the Far East. Within India, the religion split into two forms: **Theravada** and **Mahayana.** The earliest form, Theravada ('the doctrine of the elders'), spread southwards to Ceylon (now Sri Lanka) in the time of King Asoka. He ruled much of India in the middle of the 3rd century BCE, and lived a devout Buddhist life; his son and daughter were also Buddhist, and it is they who are believed to have taken the religion to Sri Lanka. From Sri Lanka, Theravada spread to Burma, Thailand and most of South-East Asia.

Sri Lankan reclining Buddha.

THERAVADA

Theravada was established as the royal religion in Sri Lanka, and became an enduring form of Buddhism. Despite incorporating some Hindu elements over the centuries, such as the increasing use of statues and the growth of shrines and priestly rites, Theravada remained essentially unchanged until Sri Lanka was colonized by the British in the 19th century CE.

Keeping close to Gautama's original teaching, Theravada frowns on ritual and images, and rejects the idea of praying to the Buddha, who has of course been subsumed in *nirvana*. To Theravadans, the universe is seen as limitless, both in time and space. A person is a temporary mixture of five kinds of impermanent states: bodily events, perceptions, feelings, dispositions and states of consciousness. All these are dispersed at death and reassembled at rebirth according to *karma,* which shows itself in thought, word and deed. Thus all actions have their consequences in the next life. For progress on the spiritual path only meditation, study, ascetic living and self-training for the purity of life are effective. The ultimate experience is not expected to involve divine vision or divine union, but contact with an ineffable, transcendental state, *nirvana.* Theravada is a prime example of mysticism without a god, or any kind of Absolute.

MAHAYANA

Mahayana Buddhism, 'the greater vehicle', developed in parallel to Theravada. Its basis was the realization that, in aiming for *nirvana,* a person was actually considering only himself and not others. This tension between the demands of inward-looking self-examination and consideration for fellow humans was ultimately resolved by the idea of the Bodhisattva, or 'Buddha-in-waiting'. Thus, as he works for his own salvation, the Bodhisattva becomes a kind of saviour, a helper of the needy in any situation.

As Mahayana grew, 'warm devotion' *(bhakti)* came to be more highly valued than the original austere self-training and mysticism. At the same time the idea arose that merit could be gained by worship *(puja)* and, to this end, more and more Buddhist statues and shrines were erected and venerated. This led gradually to accepting that grace and salvation could be obtained from outward practices as well as inward meditation.

Bodhisattva Kuan Yin,
the Chinese goddess
of mercy.

Buddhism in China

Buddhism reached China during the first century CE. Many key ideas of Buddhism complemented those of Taoism (see p. 175), which was a major influence in China at the time, for instance both religions describe themselves as a 'Path'. *Karma* and reincarnation were alien ideas, but they could easily be integrated into concepts of human and religious development. Despite encountering quite strong opposition at first, particularly from the practitioners of Confucianism (see p. 78), Buddhism gradually took root in China.

ZEN BUDDHISM

It was in China that Zen Buddhism (today especially important in Japan, Vietnam and Korea) originated, where it was called *Ch'an,* or 'meditation'.

The practice of meditation *(za-zen)* is still central to Zen as a means of reaching enlightenment *(satori);* to practise *za-zen,* followers sit in the lotus position – cross-legged, with each foot on the opposite thigh. Of equal importance with seated meditation is the *koan,* questions which require great mental struggle and have no rational answer; for example, students may be asked to describe the sound of one hand clapping. The aim is to alter one's way of thinking. The tension produced by these *koan* demonstrates Zen adherence to the power of intuition and its opposition to the

Bodhidarma, the founder of Zen Buddhism in China.

34

supremacy of reason. Words are considered superficial, and to understand the meaning of life it is necessary to delve beyond them.

TIBETAN BUDDHISM

One of the greatest Bodhisattvas is Avalokitesvara, the Bodhisattva of Compassion and the patron of Tibet. He holds a lotus in his hand. Despite China's invasion of Tibet in 1959 and the ensuing destruction of the culture, Tibetan Buddhism is showing signs of revival and has many followers in the West.

Tibetan statue of Avalokitesvara, the Bodhisattva of Compassion.

Vajrayana

Vajrayana Buddhism ('the diamond vehicle') spread east from India to Nepal and Tibet as well as to China and Japan. Vajrayana contains elements drawn from the ancient Indian philosophy of Tantrism and the original Bön religion of Tibet. Followers seek to attain realization of the absolute, using techniques such as the *mantra*. A *mantra* is a phrase repeated over and over again as an aid to meditation. '*Om mani padme hum*' is a commonly used mantra: *mani padme* means 'jewel in the lotus', while *om* and *hum* are resonant words believed to have special supernatural significance.

Other special techniques include the *mudra,* or physical gesture: Vajrayana uses many movements, especially of the hands, to express the striving for unity with the Absolute. There is also the *mandala,* or 'meditation circle', which represents cosmic relationships. Concentration on this can lead to a feeling of experiencing the divine.

Buddhism in the West

Within India, Buddhism gradually came to be assimilated into Hindu practice which has led to its virtual disappearance there as a separate religion. Now the greatest flowering of Buddhism is outside India. Buddhism, especially Zen and Vajrayana, has flourished in the West in recent decades, and in Europe, the philosopher Arthur Schopenhauer and the work of the Theosophical Society have helped to bring about a greater awareness of Buddhism. Western followers find that Buddhist teachings offer a particular wisdom not available in their own culture, especially in their aspects of tolerance, non-violence and compassion for all beings.

Buddhist Icons

The earliest statues of Buddha date from the first century CE. Before this, symbols such as Buddha's footprint or the burial mounds called *stupas* signified the person of Buddha. Statues of Buddha depict a figure with broad shoulders and long legs, symbolizing the shoulders of a lion and the legs of a gazelle. The figures are shown with special marks, particularly on the head and face, such as the *urna* in the centre of the forehead which refers to wisdom. The downcast eyes demonstrate the meditation Buddha was engaged in, and the elongated earlobes remind the faithful that to seek enlightenment they

Before the 1st century CE, footprints of the Buddha were used to represent the person of the Buddha.

must surrender worldly goods such as heavy earrings, as did Buddha, whose earlobes had stretched under the weight of gold and gemstones. The gestures of the hands of statues of Buddha each have meaning: the hand down with the palm out is the gesture for charity; the hand raised with the palm open is the gesture for reassurance. When the thumb touches the index or middle finger it is assuming the gesture for teaching.

Buddhist Monuments

Angkor Wat, deep in Cambodia, is the funeral monument of King Suryavarman II, built in the middle of the 12th century CE. It is one of the largest religious buildings in the world. At Angkor, enormous blocks of buff, ochre and pink sandstone were used to construct a huge religious complex, consisting of temples, terraces, towers and lakes. The structures were built without the use of mortar, and are covered with carvings which appear to grow from the very stones themselves. The carvings depict gods, goddesses, scenes from history and stories from the epic Sanskrit poem, the *Ramayana* (see pages 87 and 91).

The Shwe Dagon Pagoda near Rangoon, in Burma (Myanmar), is a shrine containing relics of Buddha. This sacred site is topped with many extraordinary gilded pagodas, and contains a remarkable 43-ton bell, one of the largest in the Far East.

⇜ CHRISTIANITY ⇝

- 'Christ' means 'anointed one' or 'Messiah'.
- Jesus Christ – believed to be the son of God, *c.* 6–4 BCE–CE 31–33.
- Holy book – the Bible.
- Approximately 1500 million followers worldwide.

Christians are people who acknowledge Jesus Christ as the son of God and seek to follow his teachings. They believe that Jesus lived, suffered and died as a man on earth, and that by his death and resurrection from the dead the sins of the world are paid for and so wiped away. This belief can find very different expression, and can be interpreted in many ways. At the heart of Christianity is personal faith in Jesus, the practice of prayer and contemplation, and a shared life in the Church. Christianity is the most widespread religion in the world.

Christians believe that Christ suffered, died and was resurrected from the dead to pay for the sins of the world.

The Origins of Christianity

The Life of Jesus

The Christian tradition says that Jesus was born in Bethlehem to Jewish parents and grew up in the small town of Nazareth in Galilee with his mother Mary and her husband Joseph, a carpenter. Traditionally, Christians believe that Mary was a virgin when the Holy Spirit, in the form of an angel, appeared and told her that she would bear a child who would be the Son of God.

It was estimated that when Jesus was about thirty years old, he was baptized by John the Baptist. For some years John the Baptist had been predicting the arrival of the Messiah ('Anointed One'), who would save the Jews from the oppression of foreign rulers. Jesus chose twelve companions, called his disciples, who came to believe that he was indeed the Messiah, and together they began a life of teaching and healing in Israel and surrounding countries.

Traditionally, Christ is believed to have been born in a stable in Bethlehem.

The Romans were the current rulers of Palestine, so it is likely that Pontius Pilate, the Roman Governor, considered Jesus to be a political threat, as it was claimed he would liberate the Jews. However, Jesus also claimed to be able to forgive sin, something Jewish leaders believed only God could do,

A depiction of Pontius Pilate, the Roman Governor who sentenced Christ to death.

and this claim to divinity led to charges of blasphemy. In addition, Jesus's powers of healing, in the name of God, along with his exposition of hypocrisy, challenged the beliefs of some people.

It was not long before Jesus found himself in conflict with both the Roman authorities and the Jewish leaders, and he was arrested. Jesus was tried by Pontius Pilate and it is recorded in Luke's Gospel that Pilate would have released him, but the chief priests and Jewish leaders insisted on his death. Tradition has it that Jesus was crucified alongside two common thieves on a hill called Calvary, on the outskirts of Jerusalem, and later buried in a tomb possibly belonging to one Joseph of Arimathea.

On the third day after his death Christians believe Jesus rose from the dead, and the disciples reported meeting him, speaking with him, eating with him, and touching him. They later saw him being taken up to heaven.

After Jesus's ascent to heaven, the disciples were preparing to celebrate the Jewish festival of Pentecost when, according to the book in the Bible called *The Acts of the Apostles,* 'suddenly there came a sound from heaven as of a rushing mighty wind, and it filled all the house where they were sitting. And there appeared unto them cloven tongues like as of fire .... And they were all filled with the Holy Spirit, and began to speak with other tongues, as the Spirit gave them utterance.'

This experience filled the twelve men with excitement and confidence and, now called Apostles ('sent as messengers'), they set out to spread the good news of Christ's resurrection, by preaching and teaching.

Christ on the cross.

THE FOLLOWERS OF JESUS

The Twelve Disciples (or Apostles) were Simon Peter and his brother Andrew, James and his brother John, Philip and Bartholomew, Matthew and Thomas, James, Simon, Jude and Judas Iscariot. It was Judas Iscariot who actually betrayed Jesus to the authorities; after Judas killed himself in remorse, his place as a disciple was taken by Matthias. Simon Peter (usually known just as Peter), who together with Andrew had been a fisherman until he joined Jesus, is often thought to have been the Apostles' leader. Matthew records that Jesus told Peter he would give him the keys to the Kingdom of Heaven. In Christian iconography Peter is usually shown carrying a key.

Jesus washing the feet of one of his disciples.

The Apostles Peter and Paul.

One of the most important figures among the early Christians was Saul, an educated, intelligent Jew. Some years after the Crucifixion, when Saul had been persecuting Jesus's followers, he was journeying on the road to Damascus to hunt down Christians in that city, and he saw a vision of Jesus. The vision filled him with faith in the truth of Jesus's life and teaching, and, changing his name to the Latin 'Paul', meaning 'small one', he began his mission of preaching. During the rest of his life, Paul wrote many letters (known as his 'Epistles') to the people among whom he taught, and these have survived as part of the *New Testament*. Paul's passion was to bring the message of Jesus Christ to the gentiles (non-Jews), and he was a dedicated and successful preacher. It is believed he was executed in Rome by the Emperor Nero in about CE 60.

A Growing Religion

Christianity promised eternal life and pardon from sin. Its message of personal faith and the equality of all believers before a loving God made it a very attractive option in comparison with other religions of the time. Despite bouts of savage persecution by the Roman rulers, in just over 300 years underground Christian groups took root widely throughout the Roman Empire, which at that time extended from Britain to North Africa and the Middle East. Some Jews, and many gentiles, were drawn to Jesus Christ's legacy of hope and love.

As the Apostles died, others took on the care of the early Christian groups. These first bishops and elders, as they were called, claimed that their authority was passed to them in a direct line from Jesus Christ, and as a result their rulings on religious matters became extremely important.

The word 'church' has several meanings:

- It can refer to all the Christians throughout the world: the Church.
- It can refer to the building in which Christians gather for worship: a church.
- It can refer to individual groups of Christians, such as the Anglican Church.

THE EARLY CHURCH

As more and more gentiles joined the fledgling Church, Christians began to gather for worship on Sunday, the first day of the week, rather than on Saturday, the last day of the week and the Jewish Sabbath. This was for two reasons: because Jesus Christ had risen from the dead on a Sunday and because it distinguished them from the Jews.

In CE 312 the Roman Emperor Constantine was converted to Christianity, and at last official persecution ended. Within another 100 years Christianity had become the official religion of the Roman Empire. Unfortunately, Christians in turn then became the persecutors of followers of other religions.

The Christian faith flourished as the Roman Empire sank into decadence. By the time the empire collapsed, Christianity was the dominant faith throughout its former territories. During the subsequent 'Dark Ages', the Christian Church was the bastion of learning, dominating the social, cultural and political life within Europe; no education was possible outside its auspices.

SOME EARLY CHRISTIAN SYMBOLS

- The Chi-Rho monogram. Chi (X) and Rho (P) are the first two letters of the word Christ in the Greek alphabet.
- The fish, because the letters of its Greek name *ichthus* formed an acronym of the initial letters of the Greek words for Jesus Christ, Son of God, Saviour.
- The first and last Greek letters, Alpha and Omega, symbolize God as 'the beginning and the end'.

Carving of the Chi-Rho symbol and the cross.

THE CHURCH SPLITS

The Roman Empire had four principal cities as well as its capital, Rome. These were: Jerusalem, Constantinople, Antioch and Alexandria. Gradually East and

West drifted apart politically, with Constantinople becoming the capital city in the East and Rome the capital city in the West, and the Church found itself separating also. By the 11th century CE the Church in the West (the Roman Catholic Church) and the Orthodox Church (the Church in the East) were quite distinct.

Jerusalem, one of the four principal cities of the Roman Empire.

A further separation took place in the 16th century CE, when a German, Martin Luther, called for theological and moral reforms in the Roman Catholic Church, triggering what has come to be called the Reformation. John Calvin, in Geneva, initiated another major reform,

which included the doctrine of 'predestination' which asserted that God chose in advance those who would be granted eternal salvation. The followers of Luther and of Calvin became known as Protestants, because they were protesting against the structure and teachings of the Roman Catholic Church.

Rome had become the religious centre for the Church in the West by the 11th century CE.

These new movements led to another permanent split in Christianity, and Protestant churches came to be established in many countries of northern Europe and later, with European colonialism, throughout America, Africa and Asia. A more recent movement still is that of the Pentecostal churches.

Although sharing a common Christian heritage, each church has been shaped by society and by experience, and this has led to differences both great and small. Some churches believe theirs to be the only true church and consider outsiders damned, though this belief is less common today. One important difference is the attitude each church has to the sacraments.

John Calvin, who initiated many reforms to the church, including the doctrine of predestination.

Central Themes and Beliefs

The belief common to all Christian denominations is that Jesus Christ was born, died to atone for the sins of all people, and rose from the dead to eternal life. Jesus Christ revealed God's purpose in a more complete way, promising that God is loving and forgiving, and will triumph over death. Christians believe in the return of Jesus Christ on Judgement Day, when he will rule a new world for ever, and that believers enter into the presence of God forever after death.

The Trinity

The Trinity (three aspects of one God):
- God the Father.
- God the Son.
- God the Holy Spirit.

God is infinite and one. However, through the concept of the Trinity, Christians refer to God as three persons in one: God the Father (the creator), God the Son (Jesus Christ) and God the Holy Spirit (the power of God). This expression helps to make sense of the way God is perceived, and of the influence of God that people feel in their lives. Jesus Christ is both human and divine. His incarnation as human provided a way for men and women to clarify their relationship with God and to respond to His message of love, which in turn should make it easier not to sin. Jesus Christ's death paid the punishment for the sin of all the world.

• **Sin and Atonement**

Sin is believed to be the selfish misuse of the freedom given by God, and creates a separation between God and the person who sins. Jesus atoned (paid for) human sin by his death, thereby allowing God and his people to be reunited.

The Holy Trinity – in this picture the Holy Spirit is represented by a dove.

The Practice of Christianity

Today Christianity, with all its wide family of sub-traditions, is the world's largest religion. About 1500 million people, living in almost every corner of the globe, belong to the more than 22,000 different groups within the embrace of Christianity.

There are, broadly speaking, two main groupings of Christians: **Episcopalians,** who recognize a hierarchy of priests and bishops – these include the Roman Catholic Church, the Eastern Orthodox Churches, the Lutheran Church and the Anglican Communion; and **non-Episcopalians** – these include Baptists, Congregationalists, Methodists and Reformed Churches (such as the Church of Scotland). Pentecostal churches are also non-Episcopalian.

In an Episcopalian denomination (from *episcopus* meaning 'bishop'), the principal church in a bishop's jurisdiction (known as a *diocese* or *see*) is a cathedral, its size and splendour reflecting its role as the location of the bishop's throne (*cathedra*). The bishop has responsibility for the administration of his diocese, and is also responsible for the spiritual welfare of all priests.

The non-Episcopalian denominations are generally groupings of independent congregations.

• Priesthood

All Christian church leaders are expected to serve as well as lead, and training is almost always undertaken, sometimes for several years. In the Episcopalian churches worship is led by a **priest,** a person (in Roman Catholic and Orthodox churches always a man) ordained to act as mediator between God and the congregation in administering the sacraments and preaching. In the non-Episcopalian churches the congregation appoints a **minister** (man or woman) to preach and generally lead the church. For those denominations who believe in the priesthood of all believers, whereby no intermediary is needed between God and humans, any committed Christian can lead the communion service or preach.

A priest at mass.

• **Baptism**

By means of baptism a new convert enters the life of the Church. Nearly all baptism ceremonies are based on the description of Jesus's baptism by John the Baptist, described in the Gospel of St Mark, and involve either total immersion or a sprinkling of holy water from the font. Baptism by total immersion, also called 'believer's baptism', symbolizes the washing away of sin. Baptism of babies by the sprinkling of water is normally followed, several years later, by admission into full membership of the Church.

Babies are baptized by the sprinkling of Holy Water from the font.

- **Holy Communion**

The Communion service, the central ceremony in Christian life, is known by a variety of names: *Eucharist,* the Greek word for 'thanksgiving'; *Mass;* and *The Lord's Supper.* At this service Christians recall the meals Jesus ate with his companions, share the memory of Jesus's death and resurrection, and thank God for the life of Jesus. Communicants receive bread (either a wafer or a small piece of bread) and usually a sip of wine. In most Christian churches, these items are seen as symbolic, but Roman Catholics and Orthodox Christians believe they are truly receiving the body and blood of Jesus Christ.

- **Marriage**

Although monks, nuns and Roman Catholic (and some Anglican) priests take a vow of celibacy in order to offer their whole lives to the service of God, for most Christians the marriage of one woman to one man for life symbolizes the beginning of a new family in God, and is held in high esteem.

- **Prayer**

Prayer is used to thank God for blessings, to acknowledge love, and to ask for forgiveness. It is also a method of encountering and entering into communion with God. There is no set position for prayer, but it is common in some churches to kneel. Some prayers can be spontaneous, perhaps at a quiet time, but many Christian services use standard prayers.

Sacred Texts – the Bible

The fundamental book of the Christian religion is the Bible, whose name derives from the Greek word *biblia,* simply meaning 'the books'. Written over a period of roughly 1000 years, in widely differing cultural situations and in a variety of styles and languages (based around Hebrew and Greek), the present form of the Bible was finally reached in CE 397.

The Bible consists of two separate parts: the *Old Testament,* which is similar to the Jewish Bible but interpreted differently by Christians, and the *New Testament.* The 27 books of the *New Testament* were originally written in Greek. The Roman Catholic Church includes a collection of Jewish writing called the *Apocrypha* in its version of the Bible.

A Latin Bible on a lectern.

The Bible was used in Latin for many centuries (except in the Orthodox Church, where the *New Testament* was in Greek), but was translated into German by Martin Luther (who studied the original Hebrew and Greek) in the 16th century. Since then the Bible has been translated into almost every existing language: the whole Bible is currently available in 330 languages, and the *New Testament* only in a further 770 languages. The Bible is the basis of all Church teaching, and the study of it and of the information it contains are central to Christian worship. There are, generally, two views of the Bible: one has it that it contains the literal, unalterable word of God; and the other that the Bible was written by prophets inspired by God and is therefore open to discussion and interpretation.

Other Religious Texts

In Episcopalian churches, collections of Bible readings and prayers are published to help clergy and laity to follow a sustained reading of the Bible throughout the year, and to provide outlines of worship for special services such as weddings, baptisms, funerals and feast days. Included amongst them are the *Sunday* and *Weekday Missals* (Roman Catholic), and *The Book of Common Prayer* (Anglican).

The central faiths of Christianity are contained in a 'Creed', or statement of belief, especially the 'Apostles' Creed' and the 'Nicene Creed'. One of these Creeds is usually recited during church services.

Book of Hours; these small prayer books, used for private devotions, were often lavishly decorated.

Places of Worship

Christian places of worship are many and varied. However, most church buildings of the main Eastern and Western traditions share similar features. The earliest churches were based on the shape of the Roman basilica with an oblong nave and semicircular apse. The eastward orientation derives from the pagan tradition of aligning with the direction of the rising sun, if only

to provide light for the altar. This is still observed in many denominations, but has been Christianized as looking towards Jerusalem; looking to the light also symbolizes Jesus as the Light of the World. The entrance was to be found at the opposite, western, end. Later, with the addition of a transept, the cruciform shape evolved which represents the Christian symbol itself. The area to the east of the transept, the chancel, took over the role of the apse and provided space for choir stalls and an altar. The pulpit, used in some churches, from which the congregation is addressed, stands at the corner of the north transept and chancel, with the lectern, on which the Bible rests, on the south side. The font, containing holy water for the baptism ceremony, usually stands just inside the entrance or, in Roman Catholic churches, at the front of the church.

The Christian Year

- **Advent**

The period of preparation for Christmas, and the start of the Church year.

- **Christmas**

The celebration of Jesus's birth.

- **Lent**

A forty-day preparation for Easter, corresponding to the forty days Jesus spent in the wilderness before beginning His public ministry.

- **Palm Sunday**

The first day of Holy Week, the week before Easter. It marks the day Jesus rode into Jerusalem on a donkey and was greeted by crowds throwing palm fronds in his path.

◀ *St Paul's Cathedral in London.*

- **Good Friday**
The solemn memorial of Jesus's
death on the Cross.

- **Easter Sunday**
The central Christian festival,
celebrating the resurrection
of Jesus. The date of Easter
changes each year according
to a calculation connected with
the full moon.

- **Ascension Day**
The celebration of Jesus's ascension
to Heaven, forty days after Easter.

- **Pentecost/Whitsun**
The celebration of the day when
God sent the Holy Spirit to the
Apostles, ten days after Jesus's
ascension.

- **Trinity Sunday**
The first Sunday after Pentecost,
honouring the Holy Trinity.

A Good Friday procession.

Candle used for Easter services.

Branches of the Christian Church

The Orthodox Church

- More than 140 million people are members of the Orthodox Church.

The Orthodox Church, in both Greek and Russian forms, places great emphasis upon the maintenance of tradition, and is the major Christian religious group in countries such as Russia, Armenia, Syria, Iraq, Romania, Cyprus, Serbia, Georgia and Greece. The Orthodox Church is also established in Albania, Finland, Japan, Poland and the USA and Orthodox communities exist in Australia, Uganda and Western Europe.

The Orthodox Church has no single leader analogous to the Pope (see p. 61), although the church in each nation is led by a senior archbishop called a Patriarch, and below him in the hierarchy are bishops and ordained priests, through whom God reaches the people.

Syrian Orthodox representation of the Virgin Mary and the Christ child.

Religious life centres on the Sacraments, or Mysteries, with the service of the Divine Liturgy, celebrated on Sundays and Feast Days, the most important. During the service, bread and wine is believed to be transformed into the body and blood of Jesus Christ.

Babies are baptized as young as eight days old, by total immersion. They are often dipped into the water three times, to symbolize the Trinity. This baptism admits the infant into full membership of the Church.

The Virgin Mary, or Mother of God, holds a unique position among the many saints, being deeply loved and venerated. She is believed to intercede on behalf of believers. All Orthodox services are rich in presentation, with lavish use of incense, singing, bells, candles and glowing icons, all serving to enhance the mystery and drama of the religious experience.

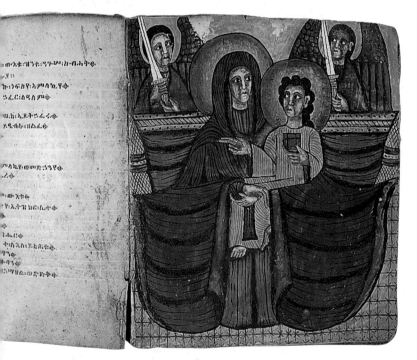

Mary and Jesus from an Orthodox Bible.

Roman Catholicism

Catholics recognize seven Sacraments, or visible signs of God's power:

- Baptism
- Eucharist
- Reconciliation
- Confirmation
- Marriage
- Ordination
- Anointing of the sick

Half the world's Christians are Roman Catholics, who number some 800 million people. The leader of the Church is the Pope, who is also the Bishop of Rome. Roman Catholics believe he derives his authority in direct descent from St Peter, whom Jesus appointed as leader of the Apostles.

Pope John Paul II.

The Pope is elected by the Sacred College of Cardinals, and leads a hierarchy of cardinals, archbishops, bishops and ordained priests, with whom he shares his ministry of teaching and leading people to God.

Roman Catholics have a firm structure of beliefs and moral codes: the 'dogma'. The emphasis is on prayer and the sacraments. Mary is venerated as the Mother of God and Queen of Heaven, she is believed to have been born without sin and to have conceived Jesus by the power of the Holy Spirit, so preserving her virginity.

Many Roman Catholic churches celebrate Mass daily. The bread and wine are believed to become the actual body and blood of Jesus Christ (this is called 'transubstantiation').

A child's First Communion is an important rite, usually taking place at about seven years of age. Confirmation, which is administered by a bishop, is usually celebrated several years after First Communion.

The authority, structure and teaching of the Roman Catholic Church, which are maintained through education and participation of members, are very clear.

The Virgin Mary with the crucified Christ.

Most of the clothes ('vestments') worn by Catholic priests at services have special names, and these also apply in the Anglican Church:

• A *cassock* is a long garment, usually black or red, worn by certain clergy and sometimes by members of a church choir.

• A *surplice* is a loose, wide-sleeved white garment, reaching to the knees, worn over the cassock.

• A *stole* is a scarf which acts as a symbol of the priesthood.

• A *chasuble* is the outer vestment worn by a priest at Mass, roughly rectangular with a hole in the middle for the head. Chasubles will almost always have a cross embroidered.

• An *alb* is a white garment worn under the chasuble, signifying the purity and holiness of the occasion.

Chasuble showing the embroidered cross decorated with the adoration of the Magi.

Bishops have two extra items:

- A *crook,* or *crozier,* is a stylized form of a shepherd's crook, symbolizing the role a bishop plays as shepherd of his flock.
- A *mitre* is the tall hat worn by bishops and cardinals, symbolizing the cloven tongues of fire which descended on the apostles on the day of Pentecost.

The Anglican Church

- Church of England established under King Henry VIII in 1534.
- *Book of Common Prayer:* reformed by Archbishop Thomas Cranmer in 1549, recast many Roman Catholic texts.

The Anglican Church, numbering approximately 55 million, is a worldwide family of autonomous churches together with the parent Church of England. It retains the threefold ministry of bishops, priests, and deacons, with bishops and archbishops appointed by the Queen on the advice of the Prime Minister in

The Anglican Book of Common Prayer.

England, and elected in other countries. Ordained by a bishop, the priest is a leader of the act of worship.

Today the Anglican Church embraces many shades of faith and practice, including Anglo-Catholic, Liberal and Evangelical. Anglo-Catholics are sometimes referred to as *High Church* and Evangelicals as *Low Church.* The Anglican Church thus offers a bridge between the Roman Catholic and the Protestant Churches.

Within recent years, and after considerable heartsearching and debate, the Church of England has admitted women to the priesthood, following the example of Anglican Churches in other countries. Some male clergy, and in a few cases their entire congregations, have joined the Roman Catholic Church in protest, but generally women priests have been welcomed.

The Virgin Mary and the infant Jesus, flanked by two saints.

Protestantism

Protestantism emphasized ways in which Christians might communicate with God, usually by reducing ritual and re-ordering liturgy, and placing less emphasis on the role of the priest as minister. One of the most important emphases was the new certainty that salvation could be by faith alone.

The Reformation was principally a movement of the Word, based upon the importance of the Bible now available to so many people through the invention of printing. It provoked a move away from ceremony, towards personal understanding and a personal relationship with God. Christians were able to read from the Bible in their own language and sermons were given a newly prominent position in church services.

The new thinking led to many different interpretations of how best to worship. All had the Bible at the centre of their worship, and most have the sacraments of baptism, marriage, and communion. Many have an organized hierarchy, with bishops and vicars ('vicar' means 'deputy'). Within the Protestant Churches there are several different shades of attitude to the Virgin Mary, with some 'high churches' differing only in degree from Roman Catholicism. Other churches offer no special reverence to Mary.

BRANCHES OF THE PROTESTANT CHURCH

• **The Lutheran Church**
The German reformer Martin Luther taught the doctrine of salvation by faith, with the authority of the Bible being attributed greater importance than church tradition; Luther translated the Bible into German, making the scriptures more accessible to the people. Preaching and music are also a central part of the faith. Today Lutherans are the main Protestant presence

Martin Luther. ▶

in Germany and Scandinavia, as well as being a worldwide presence speaking through the Lutheran World Federation. About 70 million people call themselves Lutherans. Lutheran churches are Episcopalian.

• Reformed Churches

Strongly influenced by the teachings of John Calvin (1509–1564), the Protestants of France, the Netherlands, Scotland and Switzerland preached that the authority of the Bible is paramount. One of Calvin's most characteristic teachings was that of predestination: that God has already chosen who is to be saved and who to be damned.

There are two main types of Reformed Churches: *congregational* (in which each independent local church elects its own officers, and appoints its own minister) and *presbyterian* (in which local churches group together under a regional synod of ordained presbyters and elected elders). The established church in Scotland is presbyterian, and the movement is also strong in the USA; the United Reformed Church in England is a merger of the two types. The Reformed Churches are non-Episcopalian.

FREE CHURCHES

- Baptist
- Methodist
- Society of Friends
- The Salvation Army

The 'Free Churches' are free of any link with state authority or control.

• Baptist

This movement arose at the end of the 16th century with John Smyth, who repudiated the baptism of infants, claiming that baptism is an adult declaration of faith ('believer's baptism' (see p. 52)). Today baptism is normally by total immersion. Baptist churches are independent, a loose worldwide family with great diversity of belief and practice and their worship seldom follows set liturgical patterns. The Baptist Church is particularly prominent in the USA.

• Methodist

John Wesley (1703–91) was the founder of the Methodist movement. An Anglican priest by training, Wesley experienced a spiritual enlightenment and went on to be the leader of local groups of people sharing their spiritual experiences and testimonies. The singing of hymns, and work in the community are of particular importance. Methodists are especially strong in the USA, and worldwide they number some 54 million.

John Wesley's brother Charles wrote more than 5500 hymns, among them *Hark, the Herald Angels Sing* and *Love Divine, All Loves Excelling*.

• Society of Friends

Founded by George Fox (1624–91). An early nickname for the Society was the 'Quakers', as the congregation was said to quake in awe of the Lord. Worship is mainly silent, allowing for inner communion with God. Quakers reject all the sacraments and liturgical forms, and are strongly committed to the cause of peace and to involvement in social issues.

• The Salvation Army

William Booth (1829–1912) founded the Salvation Army in 1878 as an evangelical mission to the poor in London.

The main thrust of the movement is still social work among the needy, battling against evils such as sweated labour, child prostitution and the misery caused by too much alcohol. Salvationists wear uniform and are organized into ranks like the armed forces. Worship is Bible-centred and informal, with emphasis on singing and music. There is no ordained ministry and the sacraments are not observed.

Salvation Army band procession.

The Pentecostal Movement

- Originated in USA.
- Named after the feast of Pentecost.

The Pentecostal, or Charismatic, Movement began in the early 20th century and is the very opposite of formal church worship. The feast of Pentecost celebrates the time when the Apostles felt the Holy Spirit powerfully and directly grant them 'the gift of speaking in tongues'. Pentecostalists feel they too experience the Holy Spirit personally, and believe in ecstatic religious visions, the power of healing, prophecy and speaking in tongues (either unintelligible, or echoing existing languages not apparently known to the worshipper). Acts of worship are informal and spontaneous, with everyone encouraged to call out when they feel that God urges an expression of love or faith. Sin is believed to offer a physical manifestation in illness; thus physical healing, or the casting out of devils, is seen as a cure for sin.

Today the Pentecostal Movement is especially strong, and has had a profound effect on other denominations.

Pentecost – showing the Apostles 'speaking in tongues'.

Fringe Movements

Many fringe movements are rooted in the Christian Church and, although some have only a handful of followers, others are more firmly established.

• **Jehovah's Witnesses**

Jehovah's Witnesses are an unorthodox Christian sect, founded in the USA by Charles Taze Russell at the end of the 19th century. Witnesses believe in a literal interpretation of the Bible, which is considered an infallible text. Jehovah (believed to be the correct name for God) is in conflict with Satan, and upon the imminent return of Christ, the faithful, both the living and the resurrected, will reign with Christ in the divine Kingdom on earth. Witnesses reject the doctrine of the Trinity, and forbid a priesthood. They refuse stimulants of all kinds, and will not accept surgical operations or blood transfusions, as being contrary to the word of God given in *Leviticus* 17.

• **The Church of Christ Scientist**

Founded in 1892 by Mary Baker Eddy in Boston, USA. Her system of spiritual healing was based on the principle that the mind is reality and matter illusion, and that healing can be achieved by submitting to God's grace and by correct thought. Eddy recorded her teachings in *Science and Health with a Key to the Scriptures* in 1875, a text which found a substantial readership at the time and still enjoys wide sales today.

• **The Church of Jesus Christ of Latter Day Saints ('Mormons')**

A fast-growing evangelical church. In 1827, Joseph Smith, a farmer's son from New York state, was visited by an angel named Moroni who revealed to him the whereabouts of two gold plates upon which were written the records of the

prophet Mormon. They told the
story of the journey to America of
early biblical peoples, to whom Jesus
Christ promised the establishment
of his Church in the New World.

Smith and his followers, by
now known as Mormons, moved
west. In 1847 his successor, Brigham
Young, led the group to Salt Lake
City, Utah, where a Mormon

A Mormon Tabernacle.

'empire' emerged. Utah was later incorporated into the United States. Over the
years there have been some amendments to the original tenets of Joseph Smith,
with polygamy and theocracy abandoned. However, the church has a rigid
hierarchy, and its continuing appeal lies in part in its encouragement of strong
family values and social cohesion.

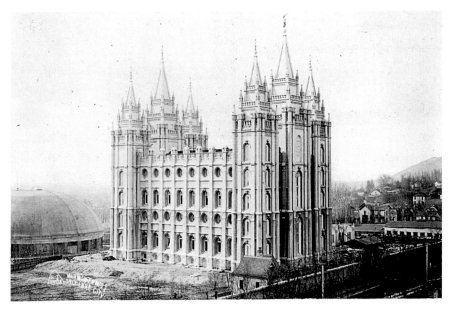

Mormon temple in Salt Lake City, Utah.

• **Unification Church**

The Unification Church was founded in Korea in 1954 by the Reverend Sun Myung Moon, whose adherents are sometimes known as 'Moonies'. The name, which is considered derisive and insulting by the group, has been used because many people consider the church to be a cult. The official name of the organization is the Holy Spirit Association for the Unification of World Christianity. The Unification Church is a highly disciplined organization, operating a network of missions, cultural undertakings, and commercial enterprises.

Reverend Moon is claimed to be the Messiah, bringing the Kingdom of Heaven to Earth. His followers believe he offers physical salvation (rather than the spiritual salvation offered by Jesus), through marriage. Moon organizes mass weddings and the children born of such marriages are believed to be free of original sin.

• **Unitarian Church**

Unitarians do not believe in the Trinity or that Jesus was divine. The origins of Unitarianism go back to the 17th century and the work of John Biddle (1615–92) though some trace it back to the early 16th century. Reason and conscience are the basis of belief and practice for Unitarians who, while believing themselves to be Christians, reject many traditional Christian doctrines. Unitarians have no formal creed.

Christianity Worldwide

The Church in China

Christianity has always been a minority influence in China. The Nestorian Church spread eastward as far as China in the first few centuries of the Christian era and was in existence when Marco Polo arrived in CE 1284. Three centuries later, the Jesuit Matteo Ricci (1552–1610) followed in the footsteps of earlier missionaries, and tried to adapt Christianity to Chinese customs and ceremonies, with little success. In the 19th century, Western traders brought further missionaries in their wake, but Christianity came to be associated with European trade and politics, and was easily suppressed. With the establishment of the Communist state in 1949, barriers to the West were raised and all religions were stifled. However, even under these harsh conditions Christianity has survived and today is one of the fastest growing religions in China.

Christian church in China.

The Church in India

Tradition has it that Christianity was first taken to India by St Thomas the Apostle. Some churches survive to display their 4th-century roots, among them sects such as Mar Thoma, Jacobite and Malabarese, but European Christianity came with the Portuguese, and particularly with St Francis Xavier (1506–52). Later, Protestant missions were more abundant when the British ruled India. Today three per cent of the population of India is Christian. The Church of South India incorporates Anglicans, Congregationalists, Methodists, and Presbyterians. The Church of North India includes all these and Baptists too.

The Church elsewhere in Asia

Roman Catholics and some Jesuit missionaries travelled as far as Japan in the 16th century, followed 300 years later by Protestants in the wake of trade and political visits by Europeans. The Philippines and Vietnam have proved the most receptive to Christianity; elsewhere the indigenous religions still prevail.

The Church in Africa

The early Christian influence in North Africa was much reduced by the upsurge of Islam, but survived mainly in Ethiopia and Egypt in the form of the Coptic Church. In the 19th century European Christian missionaries plunged deeper into Africa, with their areas of activity shadowing the political influence of the European colonial powers. Today there are numerous Pentecostal churches mixed with traditional African religions.

The Church in North and South America

In what is now the USA, the strength of different churches shadows the different areas of European influence as America was colonized. The Pilgrim Fathers brought Calvinist Protestant ethics to the East coast, and the 19th-century waves of immigration from Europe and Ireland brought Roman Catholicism, Orthodoxy and Lutheranism. The Civil War split many churches, and today there are black versions of some churches, such as the National Baptist Convention. There are also black Pentecostal movements such as The Church of God in Christ.

In Latin America, Christianity was introduced to the population by the Spanish and Portuguese conquerors in the 16th century. In some cases, when independence was won during the 19th century, anti-church feeling followed. However, the influence of the Roman Catholic Church remains strong, and in a few instances has absorbed some pre-Christian belief and ritual.

A Catholic Bishop in Haiti.

CONFUCIANISM

- Founded by K'ung Fu Tzu 551–479 BCE.
- 'Confucius' is the Latinization of K'ung Fu Tzu, which means 'Master K'ung'.
- The Four Books of Confucianism:
  The Analects of Confucius
  The Book of Mencius
  The Great Learning
  The Doctrine of the Mean
- Major influence on Chinese traditional beliefs.

The Origins of Confucianism

The roots of Confucianism long predate the birth of Confucius himself. They lie in the teachings of the ancient Chinese scholar class *(ju)*, who performed the rituals of the official cult of nature worship and ancestor reverence. They made offerings to a host of nature deities, including Heaven and Earth, as well as to the royal ancestors. Confucius always claimed to be an interpreter of these ancient scholars, not an innovator. He deliberated deeply on the meaning of tradition and was committed to parts of the past in shaping the future.

The Life of Confucius

The early family circumstances of K'ung Fu Tzu are not known, but he was certainly educated, and so was probably not among the poorest members of society. In later years, K'ung is known to have married and had children, and he appears to have been ambitious for political success, using his position to promote peace and good government. Being unable to realize this ideal in his own state, he, together with a number of his disciples, wandered for thirteen years among other states, seeking opportunities to carry out his policies. He never actually managed this but was highly successful in training young men for their own political careers, kindling in his students an enthusiasm for literature, history and philosophy, and turning them into his devoted disciples. K'ung died at the age of seventy-three.

Statue of a Confucian disciple, which stands outside the tomb of Confucius.

The Confucian Philosophy

Confucius considered himself a philosopher and teacher of ethics, rather than a religious leader, and asserted the importance of moral law. His concern was for social and political stability, which he taught could only be achieved by perfecting both social and individual life. All virtues start with family, and filial piety is the root of a good life and the beginning of a good government. Following this understanding, a book entitled the *Classic of Filial Piety* was composed, which became one of the highly favoured texts in imperial China. Ancestor worship became the centre of Confucian practices, upheld by ordinary families and the imperial household alike. Offerings were directed to ancestors, often tying in with funeral rites aimed at expressing reverence for the departed and morally educating the young.

Confucius and his followers paid great attention to the well-being of mankind and the moral quality of life. They were confident in the basic goodness of the human race and optimistic for the human future and destiny. In finding the way to order, peace and harmony, Confucians ascribed immense importance to sincerity, loyalty, and the cultivation of benevolence *(jen)*. They declared that a good leader should maintain power and order by non-violent means, by the force of moral persuasion only. By these teachings, and through the influence of the *Five Classics* and *Four Books,* the idea and practice of the scholar as administrator came to be.

Rites and Practices

Confucius underlined the sanctity of the ancient rites – including offerings to Heaven and to the ancestors – and the importance of treating all people with sincerity. He certainly believed in Heaven, the transcendental power that protected him and gave him virtue. He also recognized transcendent spiritual values, and emphasized the importance of being reverent and respectful in making sacrifices to spiritual beings. However, his attitudes towards spirits and life after death were humanistic: one could not possibly serve spirits without first serving humans, and one could not possibly understand death without first understanding life.

Perhaps the first and central concept of Confucius's teaching was the importance of 'manners' or good behaviour, *li,* which encompasses the ceremonial, or ritual, aspect of good behaviour, in its broader sense, including funerals, sacrifices, music and daily life. In these rituals Confucius saw the value of moral growth and spiritual development.

Confucius emphasized the importance of good behaviour or manners (li).

Yin and Yang

Confucianism in the Han Dynasty incorporated ideas and concepts from other schools, of which the best known are the doctrines of balance between Yin and Yang, and the classification of the world and history according not only to Yin and Yang, but also to the Five Elements: Earth, Water, Wood, Fire and Metal. Intertwined with these, and even with the popularly apocryphal writings, Confucianism was interpreted in religious, mystical and prophetic terms, and Confucius himself was taken as the 'uncrown king' [*sic* Su Wang].

For a long time after the Han Dynasty, however, the hold of Confucian doctrines over common people was weakened by the popularity of Buddhism (see p. 23) and Taoism (see p. 175). This was the case until the revival of Confucianism during the Sung Dynasty (CE 960–1279), when Neo-Confucians successfully challenged Buddhist philosophy. Buddhist and Taoist elements were incorporated into Confucian doctrines by adapting some passages in the ancient classics. This was a splendid and heroic period for Confucian scholarship. A great number of prominent Confucianists created huge and complicated doctrinal systems, thereby contributing to the absolute dominance of Confucianism in politics, ethics, literature and the general way of life in China for the next 800 years.

Symbol representing the balance of Yin and Yang, one of the best known doctrines of Confucianism.

Decoration from the House of Confucius.

The Confucian Classics

The Six Classics:
- *Shi Ching* – the Classic of Poetry
- *I Ching* – the Classic of Changes
- *Shu Ching* – the Classic of History
- *Li Chi* – the Book of Ritual
- *Ch'un-ch'iu* – Spring and Autumn Annals
- *Yueh Ching* – the Classic of Music (now lost)

The first five classics, together with some other writings, came to be used as the basis of the curriculum for the imperial college and for civil service examinations as early as in the Han Dynasty (206 BCE–CE 220). Thus a class of bureaucrats came into being who drew their learning from K'ung's ideas of moral responsibility, and placed great emphasis on correct formal behaviour and adherence to a strict moral code. In this way a classical education came to be considered central to politics. China's political life was well served by this – the concept of governing by moral example – at least in theory.

Confucianism has no church organization, priesthood, creed or dogma. Indeed, most Confucian scholars have shown little interest in a god or an afterlife. Yet, although not fully deified, Confucius has been worshipped as a superior being, the Holy and Wise Sage equal with Heaven and Earth, and prayers and sacrifices have been made to him.

HINDUISM

- One of the oldest living religions in the world – no individual founder.
- Hindu sacred texts:

  Vedas

  Ramayana

  Mahabharata
- 700 million Hindus in India, *c.* 20 million elsewhere.

The Hindu religion is deeply rooted in the culture of India and it remains the country's dominant religion. The wellspring of Hinduism is the great urban civilization of the Indus Valley, with its orderly brick-built cities, which flourished 5000 years ago.

The Origins of Hinduism

Around 1500 BCE the nomadic Aryans, the 'Noble People', swept into India from the north. With them they brought their language, Sanskrit, which is related to Latin, Greek and other Indo-European languages, and which became the sacred language of their religion. They also brought with them, among other Vedic texts (*vid* expresses knowledge), a cycle of sacred songs known as the *Rig Veda,* or Songs of Knowledge, which became sacred to Hinduism. The *Rig Veda* contains about 1000 hymns, featuring several dozen gods. Recently, however, some scholars have disputed the Aryan invasion into India, believing that the 'Aryans' were actually indigenous people and not invaders.

*Statue of Vishnu,
regarded as the preserver
of the Universe.*

The Brahmins

The Aryan priests, the Brahmins, were a class of great prestige, whose influence on the indigenous religion was profound. Masters of the sacred Sanskrit language, and experts at the elaborate rites and ceremonies, their position came to be seen as a barrier between man and god, and their dominance was called more and more into question. Around 600 BCE, Buddhism (see p. 23) and Jainism (see p. 132) arose, both coming into being partly as a revolt against priestcraft. These had a great influence on the future development of Hinduism, especially the rise of the Vedanta school.

The Vedic Tradition

Between about 300 BCE and CE 300 classical Hinduism emerged, and from this point Hinduism became less concerned with rites than with the philosophical nature of human consciousness, and with the basis of the Universe and its laws. Around this time, the *Sutras,* a collection of aphorisms which highlight the teachings of the *Veda* and the *Upanishads,* were written. This was also the time of the development of *bhakti* – devotion to only one god among the many thousands (even, some say, millions) of Hindu gods. The Vedic gods began to leave behind their old characteristics and to merge with other divinities to form new deities.

The great myths and stories of the Hindu religion were written down at this time: the *Ramayana* and the *Mahabharata* describe how history revolves like a wheel, with *dharma* (order or sacred law) prevailing; then order deteriorates into chaos until the gods begin the cycle anew.

These myths and stories help Hindus to divine a meaning and purpose in their lives, even during times of uncertainty.

Around CE 1200 a fresh wave of invaders swept in from the north. It was these Islamic attackers who, once they had subdued the country and settled in as rulers, named the faith 'Hindu' to distinguish it from their own religion. Hindu is the Persian word for 'Indian' – people of the land of the Indus River.

An illustration in the Mahabharata from Jaipur, India.

The Practice of Hinduism

Ideally, male Hindus should pass through four stages, or *ashrama,* in life:

1 student

2 householder

3 forest dweller, which denotes a time of contemplation

4 wandering holy man, or *sanyasin.*

A Holy Man.

Sacred Texts

The Hindu religion has no ecclesiastical structure or set creed, nor any single sacred book. The types of its scriptures can be broadly divided into two:

- *shruti* meaning 'heard', describing the word of God and as written in the *Vedas*.
- *smiriti* meaning 'remembered', describing works written by sages, for instance the *Ramayana* and *Mahabharata*.

- *Vedas*

The four *Vedas* are the oldest of Hinduism's sacred books, and the *Rig Veda* is the earliest and most sacred.

- *Upanishads*

These contain the philosophy known as the *Vedanta*, concerning the World Soul or *Brahman*.

- *Mahabharata*

This is a vast epic of over 100,000 couplets, written between 300 BCE and CE 300. The bulk of the text tells the story of the civil war between two branches of the ruling family, and can be read as an allegory of the fight between the forces of good and evil.

- *Bhagavad Gita* (the Song of the Lord)

This is the earliest and greatest statement of *bhakti* in Hinduism. It was originally included in the

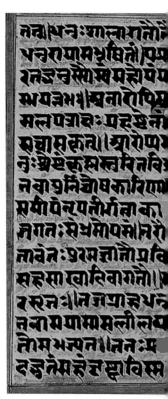

Mahabharata, and is a wonderful spiritual poem telling the story of the god Krishna and Prince Arjuna, and their part in the great battle for the kingdom of heaven. Arjuna becomes the soul of man and Krishna the charioteer of the soul, and their discourse develops a complete system of ethics, interpreting the doctrines contained in the *Upanishads.* Here *Brahman* becomes incarnate as Krishna, worthy of the love and devotion of his followers.

• *Ramayana*
Another great epic poem, this was written at the same period as the *Mahabharata,* and tells the story of Rama's rescue of his wife Sita from the demon king Ravana.

Rama's rescue of Sita.

Some Hindu Teachings

With the end of the Vedic tradition around 600 BCE came the *Upanishads,* the *Vedanta* (or the end of the *Veda*). The *Upanishads* are the texts, and the *Vedanta* is the philosophy expounded therein, the basis of Hinduism as we know it today. With the *Upanishads* came the emergence of the notion of *Brahman,* the Universal Being. *Brahman* is conceived of in two ways, either as being without form, *Nirguna Brahman,* or as having physical attributes and qualities, *Saguna Brahman.* With this came the identification of the self, or *atman,* with the Absolute, and thus with all things. This led in turn to the idea that there is only one reality, and that all things are essentially part of each other. This is the basis of Vedantic philosophy.

An important teaching of Hinduism is that the soul is born on earth many times, even though the body dies. If one has done good in a lifetime, one's new incarnation will also be good, and vice versa. This chain of cause and effect is called the law of *karma* (see Buddhism, p. 23). The ultimate aim is to escape from this cycle of life and rebirth *(samsara)* and to gain liberation *(moksha)* when the soul achieves union with *Brahman.* It is ignorance which ties humans to *samsara,* and release will be attained once ignorance is replaced by knowledge.

There are three traditional paths to achieving *moksha.* One path is the search for spiritual knowledge. This is gained through meditation, yoga and the ascetic practices associated with it, and the use of *mantras,* such as *'om',* repeated many times.

Another path is the way of duty and performing good works, as well as the fulfilment of obligations. The path of *bhakti,* or devotion, is also accepted as a means of achieving liberation. Because the idea of *Nirguna Brahman* can appear so impersonal, even distant, many people find it easier to make a commitment to a single god personifying one aspect or function of *Brahman*. As all gods within Hinduism are understood as expressions of *Saguna Brahman,* each is seen as offering a different way of approaching the Absolute. This path leads to the idea that salvation is a gift from God rather than a human achievement.

Illustration showing the various incarnations of Vishnu.

Hindu Worship

In India, Hindu shrines may be simple structures in the home or at the roadside, perhaps containing just one image, but the most important temples are magnificent structures of elaborately carved

An elaborate Hindu temple in Delhi.

stone and wood. Each temple is dedicated to a specific god, and at the same time functions as a symbol of the whole cosmos.

Devotion is expressed in acts of worship, or *puja*. Worship in Aryan times concentrated on a sacred fire and was usually held out of doors. The idea of temple worship was probably a feature of the Indus Valley people.

Worshippers are required to undertake ritual acts of purification before approaching the divinity. These rites might include washing, often to the accompaniment of hymn-singing, the ringing

Washing is one of Hinduism's ritual acts of purification.

of bells, and the burning of incense. The worshipper will then pay his or her respects to the god and make an offering of money or some other gift. Priests might read from the scriptures to an assembly of worshippers, but generally, worship is an individual act, and for this reason rites performed in the home are of equal significance.

Most homes contain a shrine, however small, and often a special room will be put aside for *puja*. The shrine will have a picture, perhaps an image of the chosen god, and flowers, incense and coloured powders. Worship is usually a daily routine, both morning and night, involving purification and prayer.

Hindu communities outside India often convert buildings such as

Shiv Mandir temple in Varansi, one of Hinduism's Holy Cities.

large houses or even disused churches for use as temples; however, in Spring 1995 the stunning Swaminarayan Mandir temple opened in London, England – the first traditional Hindu temple ever constructed of stone in Europe, and the largest outside India.

Most large temples are built to a long-established design and have an outer wall within which there may be small separate shrines. Worshippers remove their shoes at the entrance to the temple complex where there is sometimes a bell to be rung. Inside, statues of gods and goddesses line the walls leading to the lamp-lit main image, above which rises a tall tower.

Hindu temples are richly decorated with sculptures, each with a precise iconographic meaning and a role in identifying the principal deity within the temple. Many of the gods represented by these sculptures share similar, idealized physical features, and can be distinguished from one another by the objects they hold, their clothing and ornaments. An example of this is Ganesh, the son of Shiva. In three of his four hands he is shown holding a rosary, a snake (showing his control over death) and a broken tusk. His fourth hand is held up to bless his devotees.

The four-armed elephant god, Ganesh.

Hindu Gods

The three main Hindu gods are:

- *Brahma,* the creator
- *Vishnu,* the preserver (also known as Krishna)
- *Shiva,* the destroyer.

Hindus believe that God descends to earth whenever there is an increase of evil; these incarnations are called *avatars.* Traditionally there are 10 *avatars,* the most popular being Krishna, the *avatar* of Vishnu and hero of many myths as lover, warrior and king. Krishna was once a cow-herd, and partly for this reason cows are now sacred throughout India.

Shiva, the destroyer, is often shown as Lord of the Dance, performing the dance of creation. He is shown standing on the back of the dwarf of ignorance, with his left leg poised dramatically in the air. The position of Shiva's hands, the objects he holds, and the ornaments he wears all explain the significance of the dance.

Statue of Shiva dancing in a circle of flames.

Man dressed as Hanuman, the monkey god.   *Statue of Kali (in the foreground).*

Other popular deities are:

- *Ganesh,* the elephant-headed god, the remover of obstacles.
- *Lakshmi,* the goddess of fortune and beauty.
- *Kali,* Shiva's consort, bringer of disease and war. Kali is also known as Parvati and Durga.
- *Hanuman,* the monkey god.

The Caste System

The social groups with which Hindus identify most strongly are their *jatis* or castes, and this system is the basis for traditional social divisions in India. A caste is a hereditary group whose members marry only among themselves. Each has its own origin myth, traditional occupation, diet, rules relating to kinship, and various forms of behaviour.

The caste, or *varna*, (*varna* means 'colour') came out of the original creation myth, in which Indra brought existence out of non-existence, and grouped all things according to divine intention. Originally the notion of *varna* and caste were distinct. Caste plays an important part in the traditional life of India, especially in villages, where about 75 per cent of the population lives. Here caste will determine employment, marriage and consequent economic status. The higher castes are referred to as twice born and bound up with this is the idea of contamination: to touch a person of a lower caste demands a subsequent act of ritual purification. Discrimination on the basis of caste was made illegal in India in 1947.

According to generally accepted beliefs associated with reincarnation, or rebirth after death, the caste into which one is born depends on one's karma – that is, one's accumulated good and bad deeds in previous existences. The way to achieve higher status in future incarnations is to perform one's duties, *dharma,* according to caste expectations. By performing one's duties, one may eventually achieve *moksha,* release from the continuous round of rebirths.

There are four traditional caste divisions, within which there are many sub-divisions *(jati):*

Brahmins form the priest class.

Kshatriyas form the warrior and ruler class.

Vaishyas form the farmer and commercial class.

Shudras form the artisan and servant class.

Untouchables are outside the caste system. Today, many Hindus are against the idea of people being considered untouchable.

Members of the top three castes usually wear a sacred thread looped over the left shoulder and hanging to the right hip.

A Brahmin practising yoga.

The Spread of Hinduism

Modern Groups Based on Hinduism

Hindu culture has exercised widespread influence outside India, particularly in South-East Asia, but wherever Indians went their religion went too. Latterly, this has been to Africa and America as well as to the United Kingdom, where Indian religious thought and practice have been widely disseminated.

TRANSCENDENTAL MEDITATION

Maharishi Mahesh Yogi first came to Britain in 1958, but it was not until his followers included the Beatles, who joined him at the end of the 1960s, that Transcendental Meditation (TM) came to be widely known and practised. TM draws upon Yogic Sutras and elements of the Indian idea of rebirth. By exploring the depths of self and of consciousness it aims to improve the life of the practitioner, and thereby the life of the whole community.

Meditators use a secret *mantra,* a mystical verse of Indian scripture, given to them by their Guru on their initiation, as an incantation. Their spiritual journey proceeds by way of lessons and ever more demanding techniques.

INTERNATIONAL SOCIETY FOR KRISHNA CONSCIOUSNESS (ISKCON)

In 1965, at sixty-nine years of age, His Divine Grace A. C. Bhaktivedanta Swami Prabhupada went to the USA to spread God's word. His message of a state of bliss, attainable through sincere devotional practices, became instantly popular – more so when one of the Beatles, George Harrison, took a much-publicized interest.

Krishna devotees in a temple.

The Swami translated and annotated the *Bhagavad Gita,* which he believed to be a literal record of God's word. Serious adherents of the Society eschew stimulants, meat, and sex outside marriage. Bands of devotees are to be seen singing, chanting, and dancing through many city streets, wearing their distinctive saffron-coloured robes, the men with their heads shaved, except for the topknot (the *sikha,* by which Krishna will pull them up to heaven). They

are popularly known as the 'Hare Krishna' sect, after their mantra, which begins 'Hare Krishna, Hare Krishna…'.

Despite internal difficulties since the Swami's death, the movement continues to attract followers both in the West and in the East.

Followers of Krishna dancing in a city street.

DIVINE LIGHT MISSION

The Guru Maharaji arrived in London in 1971, bringing with him the Divine Light Mission, a movement which had been organized by the Guru's father in India in 1960. He taught four simple meditation techniques which facilitate self-understanding and communion with the inner soul, and ultimately the perception of those characteristics of the soul described as 'Divine Light', 'Music', 'Nectar' and 'Holy Name'.

The movement continues despite financial difficulties and power struggles within the leadership. The name was recently changed to *Elan Vital.*

Hindu Festivals

Hinduism has many holidays, some celebrated by the majority of Hindus and others only by certain communities, or under special circumstances. Most of the holidays are based on the Hindu calendar, which originated in ancient India.

- **Diwali**

The Festival of Light, marks the New Year, and falls in October. People light candles or lamps in their windows to welcome Rama home to his kingdom as rightful king. Lakshmi, the goddess of wealth, is also worshipped on Diwali, and many businesses open new account books at this period.

- **Dussehra**

This festival celebrates the triumph of good over evil, and frequently involves the acting out of the story told in the *Ramayana.*

• Holi

Holi falls at the start of India's hot season in February, and is a joyful time dedicated to Krishna. People throw coloured water and bright powders at each other, with no barriers of rank or caste. All the colours will wash off in the evening, and then comes a time of visiting friends and exchanging good wishes and sweetmeats.

Lighting candles during Diwali.

Hindu Weddings

Many Hindu marriages are arranged by the parents, the intention being that the marriage is between two families as well as two individuals. The date is set by the priest after he has studied the stars for the most auspicious time, and the ceremony is performed before a special fire, accompanied by hymns and offerings. The groom usually arrives on horseback, dressed in bright colours and garlanded with jasmine and roses.

Festival of Holi.

❧ ISLAM ❧

- The Prophet Muhammad ﷺ born CE 570 in Makkah (Mecca).
- *Islam* means peace through compliance with Allah's divine guidance.
- Holy book – The *Qur'an*.
- Approximately one thousand million followers.

The Essence of Islam and its Meaning for Believers

Islam is known as the *Din-al-Fitrah* or 'natural way', and takes full account of all aspects of human nature. One meaning of the Arabic word *Islam* is 'peace', a peace attained through willing obedience to Allah's divine guidance. This 'way of peace' teaches that to be entirely at one with, and doing no harm to, any of Allah's creation – animal, vegetable or mineral – one must become 'like a feather on the breath of God'.

The Conventions

ﷺ this Arabic 'logo-type' is composed of the words *Salla-llahu alayhi wa sallam* – peace and blessings of Allah upon him. They are used by Muslims every time the Prophet Muhammad ﷺ is mentioned.

السلام This Arabic 'logo-type' is composed of the words *Alayhi salaam* – peace be upon him. They are used by Muslims after the names of prophets are mentioned. Many will also say this after mentioning any of the twelve Imams descended from the Prophet Muhammad ﷺ.

'Allah' is the Islamic name for the One True God. Used in preference to the word God, this Arabic term is singular, has no plural and is not associated with masculine, feminine or neuter characteristics.

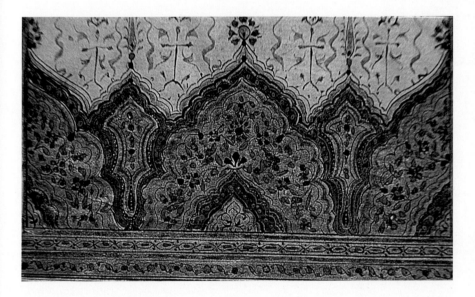

Details from an illuminated prayer book – "In the name of Allah, the most merciful, the beneficent".

The Origins of Islam

There are over a thousand million Muslims throughout the world. Muslims (meaning 'those who have accepted Islam') trace the roots of Islam to the creation of the first man, Adam 🕮, the first of a line of many prophets. Their function was to fulfil Allah's promise to Adam 🕮 when He gave the reassurance that He would not leave people on earth without guidance.

Through their own example, Prophets and Messengers gave guidance to people as to how they should behave towards every aspect of Allah's creation, and how to worship the Creator. Allah's messengers included Nuh 🕮 (Noah), who by reasoning with people worked to eradicate injustice; Ibrabim 🕮 (Abraham), who with his son Ismail 🕮 built the *Ka'bah* (now within the sanctuary in the Grand Mosque) in Makkah and invited people to come there for the worship of the One True God; Musa 🕮 (Moses), who led his people out of oppression and was given divine religious laws, the Tawrah *(Torah),* by which they should live; and Isa 🕮 (Jesus), who was born of a virgin as a sign and a mercy for humankind. In time, people forgot, ignored or changed their teachings to suit themselves. Muslims believe that the final prophet, Muhammad 🕮, was sent by Allah to bring previous prophetic missions to perfection, and to complete divine religious laws which will remain valid until the end of time.

The Life of Muhammad ﷺ

In 6th-century CE Arabia, the majority of people were pagans. They lived in tribes, each with its own leader. Some were farmers, others traders, but many reared camels and raided other tribes for booty. Makkah had become a wealthy trading centre, Ibrahim's ﷺ teaching had been forgotten, and the *Ka'bah* was now full of idols. Many leading citizens encouraged pilgrimage, and profited from those who came to worship the idols.

It was into this society, in CE 570, that Muhammad ﷺ was born in Makkah. His parents died and he was looked after first by his grandfather and then by his uncle. As he grew up, Muhammad ﷺ became known as Muhammad al-Amin, 'the trustworthy'. He worked for a wealthy older widow, Khadijah, who, impressed with his honesty, asked him to marry her. He was twenty-five, and they remained married until her death twenty-five years later.

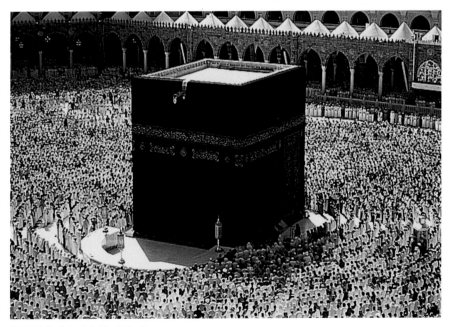

The Ka'bah in Makkah during prayer.

Muhammad ﷺ often used to go from the bustle of Makkah for periods of reflection in a cave outside the city. During one such time, when he was forty years old, he heard the voice of the angel Jibril giving him a command.

'Recite in the Name of your Lord who creates,
Creates man from a clot.
Recite! Your Lord is the Most Bountiful,
Who taught the use of the pen,
Taught humankind that which they knew not.'

Qur'an 96:1–5

Muhammad ﷺ repeated the words until he had learned them by heart. He rushed home and related his experience to his wife, who comforted and reassured him. Khadijah and the Prophet's young cousin Ali ﷺ were the first people to understand and accept that Allah had chosen 'the trustworthy one' to deliver his final guidance. Muhammad ﷺ continued to receive revelations for over twenty years.

PROPHETHOOD

As time passed, it became clear to ever-increasing numbers of people that Muhammad ﷺ was indeed a Messenger of Allah. The least receptive were those powerful Makkans who trafficked in idols and slaves and benefited most from idol worship and the pilgrim trade. They treated Muhammad ﷺ with derision. Despite this, he continued to deliver the revelations of Allah's mercy and justice, which were welcomed by the poor and oppressed.

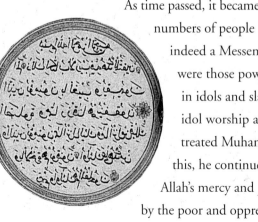

Arabic script from a Qur'an.

His opponents saw that ridicule and sarcasm were not enough to stop him, and since he refused to accept their bribes, they resorted to open persecution. His followers were tortured and punished. The Prophet ﷺ sent some of the growing Muslim community to Abyssinia to find relief from the harassment. Despite emissaries from the ruling Makkans demanding their return, the Abyssinian ruler gave them sanctuary.

Exasperated by the Prophet's ﷺ condemnation of idol worship, and his challenge to their cruel customs and immoral and materialistic way of life, the Makkans finally declared a ban on all relations with Muslims. The Prophet ﷺ, his family and followers were driven from Makkah. For three years they sheltered in a valley outside the city in conditions of hardship and hunger, until the solidarity of their opposition broke down and they were able to return to their homes.

Minarets of the Prophet's ﷺ Mosque.

THE MIGRATION TO MADINAH

The deaths of both his wife Khadijah 🕮 and uncle Abu Talib, prominent people whose position had afforded him some protection, exposed Muhammad 🕮 to further persecution. As this increased, the leaders of Madinah (Medina), a city north of Makkah, invited Muhammad 🕮 to make the city his home. Narrowly escaping assassination in Makkah he travelled to Madinah in CE 622. The migration from Makkah to Madinah, known as the *Hijrah,* became the starting point of the Muslim calendar.

Muhammad 🕮 was very well received in Madinah where he became head of what was to become the first Islamic state. Here, the Friday congregational prayer was initiated, the month of *Ramadan* fixed as the month of fasting, and the *Ka'bah* at Makkah declared the direction to be faced by Muslims while praying.

The Ka'bah in Makkah, towards which all Muslims must pray.

THE ACCEPTANCE OF ISLAM

The years at Madinah were a time of development and growth for the Muslim community, a time for them to learn the teachings of the *Qur'an* as it was being revealed, and to follow the peerless example of Muhammad ﷺ. For eight years, until they realized that they could not destroy Islam by military means, the Makkans regularly engaged the Muslims in battle. This ended with the treaty of Hudaybiah, and Muslims were finally able to declare their faith without harassment. The Islamic teachings of justice and fairness, brotherly love, respect for others and mercy to the weak, called upon people to abandon ignorance and superstition, to read and to seek knowledge.

In CE 630, Muhammad ﷺ and his followers entered Makkah and immediately granted their Makkan enemies a general amnesty. At the *Ka'bah*, Muhammad ﷺ cleared the hundreds of idols from inside and proclaimed that truth had come and falsehood had vanished.

Tribes from near and far sent delegations to proclaim their acceptance of Islam and the Prophet Muhammad ﷺ as their leader. In CE 632, Muhammad ﷺ returned to Makkah to perform what has become known as the 'Farewell Pilgrimage'. Three months after his return to Madinah, he died (Peace and blessings of Allah be upon him). He was 63, and by the time of his death the majority of people in Arabia had accepted Islam as their way of life.

'Allah' – Brass plate on the Dome of the Rock in Jerusalem.

Leadership of the Ummah After the Prophet ﷺ

After the death of Muhammad ﷺ, concerns arose about who would lead the Muslim community. It is recorded in Islamic tradition, and people were aware, that the Prophet ﷺ had frequently and publicly named Ali ؑ, his cousin and son-in-law, as his successor. But immediately following the Prophet's death, while Ali ؑ was still occupied with burial arrangements, some Muslims nominated and chose Abu-Bakr, a friend and companion of Muhammad ﷺ, as the new leader. Abu-Bakr was known as the Khalifah and he was followed in leadership by three other companions of Muhammad ﷺ. All four of them are known as the Rightly Guided Khalifahs; the last of these was Ali ؑ.

Medallion on the interior wall of Al-Aqsa mosque in Jerusalem, showing the word 'Ali' in Arabic script.

The Division of Islam

THE IMAMATE

The followers of Ali ﷺ – Shi'at Ali (these followers are known as Shi'ah Muslims) – believe that the guardianship of the faith resided with the Ahl-ul-Bayt (specific members of the family of Muhammad ﷺ) who had been divinely appointed by Allah to provide error-free guidance to the Muslim community. These leaders became known as the Imams. Unlike Muhammad ﷺ, they were not given the quality of Prophethood or the ability to receive revelation. Shi'ah Muslims believe that without the continuity, guidance and leadership of the Imams, the essence of Allah's final message would have been lost, disrupted or subverted, as happened with the warnings of earlier prophets.

An Imam leader addressing a congregation.

THE KHALIFATE

Since the time of the first four Khalifahs, the Muslim world has never come under the rule of one single leader, accepted by all. Self-proclaimed Khalifahs, however, ruled over their own nation states.

Sacred Text – the *Qur'an*

The word *Qur'an* means 'that which is recited'. At different times and at different places over a period of twenty-three years, Allah's message was

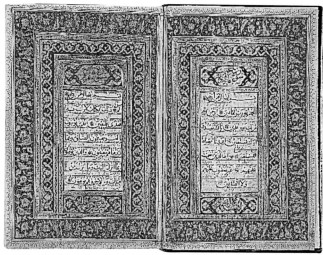

revealed (in the Arabic language) to Muhammad ﷺ by the angel Jibril. Each year during the month of Ramadan, Muhammad ﷺ recited to the angel all that he had been taught, to ensure that he had memorized it correctly. By the

The Qur'an.

time of his death all the revelations had been written down to form the *Qur'an*. The *Qur'an* is the final revealed words of Allah for the guidance of humanity, unchanged since the time of its revelation. It is not written for any single race or class of people, but is addressed to all people, everywhere, and is continuously relevant. In its own words, it is addressed to 'people who think' and 'people who use their reason'. The *Qur'an* helps people understand their situation and role on Earth. It makes a clear distinction between good and evil and establishes basic principles of law which reinforce moral teachings. The *Qur'an* has a truly awesome significance for all Muslims.

The moral code and values of Islam taught in the *Qur'an* are derived from the Creator as 'Ethical Being' with the best attributes. Muslims regard the *Qur'an* as the very words of their Creator, His explanations and directions to all humankind on how to keep to the straight safe way. Muslims believe the *Qur'an* to be the way to success and security, through peaceful coexistence with every other element of His creation.

The *Qur'an* is not, however, a menu from which to pick and choose. Regarding it as 'the Maker's handbook for living', Muslim believers have no option but to accept all the guidance in the *Qur'an*. They cannot simply drop parts they do not like. For both the two main branches of Islam, *Shi'ah* and *Sunni*, the moral absolutes and religious values in the *Qur'an* are the basis of all moral reference.

The whole *Qur'an* is arranged in 114 *Surahs,* each consisting of a number of *Ayats* (literally 'signs') in Arabic. To make it easy to read, the text of the *Qur'an* is divided into thirty equal parts for those who wish to read the whole of the *Qur'an* in daily sections over a month; or seven equal parts for those who wish to read the whole *Qur'an* in one week. The *Surahs* and *Ayats* of the *Qur'an* are used in *Salah* as part of the five daily prayers.

The learning and teaching of the Qur'an is an essential part of Muslim life.

The Qur'an was recited to Muhammad ﷺ by the angel Jibril.

The Qur'an is central to Islamic faith and is read, pondered, understood, applied and obeyed. Through the Qur'an, Allah stresses knowledge and reason as the valid way to faith and consciousness of Him. As a result, the Qur'an is one of the most widely and frequently read books in the world, and is available in almost every written language. There are thousands of Muslims who can recite the entire Qur'an from memory.

Sudanese Muslims praying towards Makkah.

Practices of Islam
Sunnah

Muslims love Muhammad ﷺ and try to live up to his example and to follow his *Sunnah* – customs and tradition and the model practice of his way of life – these are a permanent source of guidance for all aspects of their lives, practical, moral and spiritual. The manner in which Muslims eat, dress or enter a house is influenced by the *Sunnah*. The principal sources of knowledge about the *Sunnah* are the *Hadith:* these are reports of the sayings and deeds of the Prophet Muhammad ﷺ, as recounted by his household, progeny and companions. They are a major source of Islamic law. To be included in a collection of *Hadith,* both the reports of what Muhammad ﷺ said or did, and the character of the narrators of each report, were thoroughly examined and verified by corroborative reports.

The Dome of the Rock, Jerusalem.

Shari'ah

The code of conduct for Muslims, based upon the *Qur'an* and *Sunnah*, is known as the *Shari'ah* – Islamic regulations, principles and values from which the law and legislation are formed. Because it is Allah's law, it is permanent for all people at all times. It is not subject to political changes or variations in moral standards. All its basics are firm and settled, but new circumstances can be flexibly responded to by those knowledgeable in *Qur'an* and *Sunnah*.

'O you who believe! Be always upright for the sake of Allah, and bear witness with justice. Do not let the hatred of a people incite you to behave inequitably. Act equitably. That is nearer to piety.'

Qur'an 5:8

'The Prophet ﷺ said, "The highest level of justice is to love for people whatever you love for yourself and hate for them that what you hate for yourself."'

Hadith

The *Shari'ah* covers all aspects of human life, spiritual and social, including faith and moral conduct, acts of worship, family and international relations, business

and economic life, social and political affairs, crime and punishment, international law and military affairs. The principal purpose of *Shari'ah* is to bring justice to everyone through the creation of a morally responsible society.

Illustrated pages from the Qur'an.

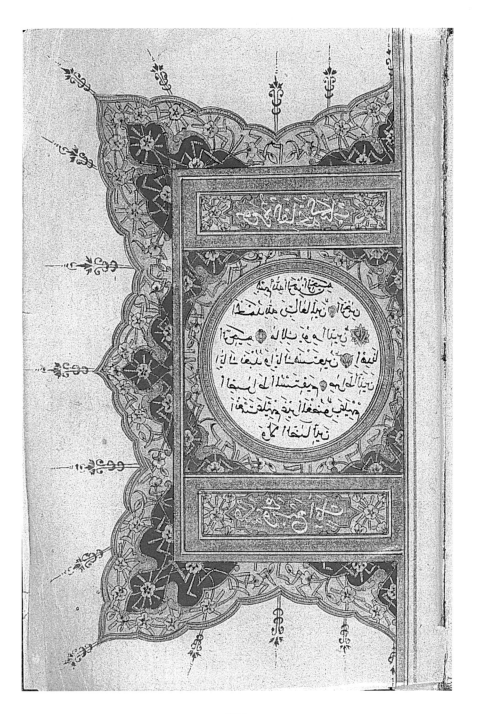

Groups within Islam

The two branches of Islam are **Shi'ah** and **Sunni** of whom the Sunni are in the majority. All Muslims share belief in the teachings of the *Qur'an*; face towards the *Ka'bah* in Makkah in prayer; and strive to follow the teaching and example – the *Sunnah* – of the Prophet Muhammad ﷺ.

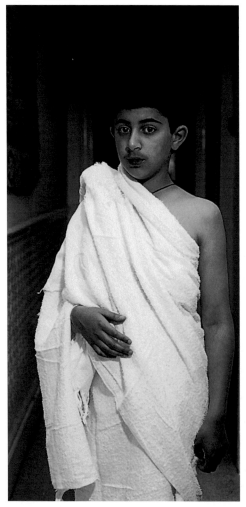

According to Sunni understanding, the five pillars of Islam are:

- the declarations that 'There is no god but Allah, and Muhammad ﷺ is His Messenger'.
- *Salah* – the daily five prescribed times of formal worship.
- payment of *Zakat* – welfare due.
- pilgrimage during the month of *Hajj*.
- fasting during the month of *Ramadan*.

According to Shi'ah understanding, the beliefs of Islam are likened to the roots of a tree and the religious practices to its branches.

Boy dressed for pilgrimage.

Five beliefs lie at the root of the Islamic religion:
- the Oneness of Allah
- the Justice of Allah
- prophethood
- divinely guided leadership
- the Day of Judgement.

These central beliefs are the basis for ten religious practices:
- *Salah*
- *Sawm* – fasting during the month of *Ramadan.*
- *Hajj* – pilgrimage.
- *Zakat*
- *Khums* – contribution of one fifth of surplus annual income.
- *Jihad* – striving to overcome the desires of one's ego.
- enjoining good.
- forbidding evil.
- love for the divinely guided leaders.
- avoiding enemies of the divinely guided leaders.

Prayer outside the mosque in Regent's Park, London.

Irfan – Sufism

A Sufi is a Muslim who tries to come closer to Allah. People intent on achieving this are known as Arifs (gnostics), the adepts of Irfan *(gnosis)*. They worship Allah not for reward, nor because they are afraid of Him, but because they know and love Him. Both Sunni and Shi'ah Muslims may follow the way of Irfan. Knowledgeable and highly respected teachers guide a large proportion of Muslims, throughout the world, to follow the spiritual path to perfection via constant remembrance of Allah.

Ramadan

Ramadan is the ninth month of the Islamic lunar calendar and its start depends on the sighting of the new moon. Muslims fast for all of the 29 or 30 days of this month. Fasting as ordered by Allah in the *Qur'an* means that from before dawn until sunset, Muslims refrain from all food and drink including water, and make special efforts to guard against every kind of bad behaviour. In addition, during these hours, people also fast from many normally permitted actions such as marital relationships.

For believers, the principal purpose of Ramadan is to focus attention on, and promote greater awareness of Allah. This is a month of intense devotion, during which the *Qur'an* was revealed. Muslim communities draw closer as they experience an increase in self discipline,endurance and compassion for those in need. Fasting is not a penance for sins nor is it a means of appeasing Allah.

The very old, the infirm, the mentally ill, and pregnant women, nursing mothers and children below the age of puberty are not required to fast. Young people learn to fast progressively: little children may fast until midday and extend this time as they grow older.

On Id-ul-Fitr, the first day of the succeeding month of Shawwal, Muslims attend Id Salah at the mosque, celebrate the end of the fast and are forbidden to fast on this happy occasion. It is however a tradition to fast a further six days during Shawwal.

Hajj is the annual pilgrimage to Makkah undertaken from the eighth to the thirteenth day of Dhul-Hijjah, the twelfth month of the Islamic lunar calendar. To complete Hajj once in a lifetime is ordered by Allah and is therefore compulsory for every adult Muslim who has the health and the means. Pilgrimage takes place in Arabia as the pilgrims move from Makkah to Arafat, to Muzdalifah, to Mina and to Makkah again. Pilgrims renew their links with, and re-enact important events in, the lives of the Prophets Ibrahim ﷺ, Isma'il ﷺ and Muhammad ﷺ (peace and blessings upon them all) and Hajar, the mother of Isma'il ﷺ. Hajj is a profound demonstration of the unity of Islam and its egalitarian nature. All men are dressed alike in two unsewn white sheets. Women wear their normal loose modest clothing which covers all but their faces and hands. Above all Hajj is a journey of individual self renewal inspired by devotion to and consciousness of Allah Almighty.

Muslim pilgrims in Makkah.

The Spread of Islam

Wherever Muslims settle, they should accept and assimilate social and cultural customs which do not conflict with Islamic teaching.

In the hundred years after the death of the Prophet Muhammad ﷺ, Islam spread to North Africa and Central Asia. Through trading links with Arabian seamen, Islam became established in India in CE 711. By the 16th century, India was ruled by the Mogul Empire, with Agra at its capital. Although the Emperor Akbar was a Muslim, most of the people of India were Hindu. Because of this he ordered Muslims not to kill cows, which Hindus considered sacred, and he made a Hindu his second in command.

Negri Sembilan State Mosque in Seremban, Malaysia.

From India, Islam spread to South-East Asia, Malaysia, Indonesia and the Philippines through Muslim missionaries and traders. An attraction of Islam is that it has no caste system and frees people from the social class or occupation of their forefathers.

GREAT CITIES OF THE ISLAMIC WORLD

By the 9th and 10th centuries CE, the greatest city in the ever-expanding Islamic world was Baghdad. Here, through contact with China, the art of paper-making flourished. The resulting production of books greatly encouraged the spread of literacy and knowledge of Islam.

Islam spread early into Central Asia. Trade from the Eastern Mediterranean to China helped to spread Islam all along the silk route. Samarkand, in the heart of Central Asia, developed as a remarkable and beautiful city. Ulugh Beg, its ruler, built a huge observatory and wrote an encyclopedia on the courses, positions and altitudes of stars. Astronomy and navigating by the stars were important for travelling Muslims to be able to work out the direction of Makkah and the start of the lunar month.

In the 10th and 11th centuries CE, Cordoba, the capital of Muslim Spain, became the most

Interior of the Hassan Mosque, Cairo.

splendid city in Europe. There was street lighting, many homes had running water and for those which didn't there were hundreds of public baths. European scholars came to Spain to study under the great masters such as ibn Rushd and ibn al-Arabi. The development of Islamic knowledge in Spain was an important factor in the renaissance in Europe several centuries later.

The city of Constantinople became Istanbul and was developed by the Sultan Mehmet II into the capital of the Ottoman Empire. He invited persecuted Muslims and Jews from Spain and other parts of Europe to make their homes there. Through the Ottoman Empire, roads and rest houses were built to assist travellers. There was also an efficient system of legal and social services to help people. In 1560, the mosque complex of the Sulimaniyyah – which included seven colleges, a hospital, an asylum, a soup kitchen, a bathhouse, schools, shops, a sports ground and fountains – was completed.

Belief in the equality of people was a factor in the spread of Islam to the West African countries of Mali, Senegal, Nigeria and Ghana from the 8th to the 18th centuries. The city of Timbuktu grew up and developed

Mosque of Suleiman the Magnificent in the Sulimaniyyah complex, Istanbul.

Traditional Qur'anic School, Sudan.

around its mosque as the greatest centre of learning south of the Sahara. The *Qur'an* schools, which its students then opened throughout West Africa, continue teaching Islamic studies to this day.

MOSQUES

As the Islamic way of life flourished, Muslims on every continent built mosques as the heart of their communities. Outside, they often looked just like the buildings around them. Whether made from marble or mud brick, however, they all have similar features inside, and a large open area to pray in. This mosque space is designed to create a sense of peace. Architecture and town planning became well developed in Islamic societies, with mosques and colleges physically and spiritually central to development.

Interior of the Al-Aqsa mosque in Jerusalem.

Islam in the World Today

During the 19th century, the Ottoman Empire, which ruled so much of the Islamic world, was under threat from colonial powers. By the end of the First World War, France, Britain, Russia, Holland and Italy ruled nearly all the countries of North, West and East Africa and the Middle East, as well as India, South-East Asia and Central Asia.

These colonial powers put their own European and Christian-based legal, social and government administrative systems in place of the existing Islamic ones. During the 20th century, however, the process of decolonization has seen a desire for the return to Islamic systems in these countries.

As a result of the connections made between Europe and the Islamic world, large numbers of Muslims have settled in Europe. Along with the ever-increasing numbers of converts to Islam, they now make up the second-largest

Great emphasis is placed on science in the Islamic studies.

religious community in
Europe. At the turn of
this century, thousands
of Muslims moved from
the Middle East to settle in
South America and work as
traders. There are about a
million and a half Muslims
in South America, while in
the United States there are
over six million.

In many Muslim-
majority countries,
Muslims are working to
re-establish the teachings
and institutions of Islam.
International Islamic
organizations provide a
network of communication

Shoe rack at the Prophet's Mosque.

and support to benefit all those in need through the *ummah* – the world-wide
community of Muslims. Wherever they live, Muslims are guided by what Allah
teaches in the *Qur'an:*

'Mankind. We created you from a single pair of a male and a female,
And made you into nations and tribes, that you may know each other
(Not that you may despise each other). Truly, the most honoured of you
in the sight of Allah are those who are the most righteous.'

Qur'an 49:13

❧ JAINISM ❧

- Followers of *Jina* ('conqueror'), 599–527 BCE.
- Two schools of Jainism: *Svetamabaras* and *Digambaras.*
- Approximately 7 million Jains worldwide, 30–35 thousand in the UK.

Jains believe that the world and everything in it is subject to growth and decline on an infinite cosmic wheel. Their lives are a struggle for liberation from this cycle of rebirth, towards a strenuously achieved bliss.

Lord Mahavira, the last of the twenty four Jinas.

The Origins of Jainism

The origins of Jainism lie in the centuries leading up to the 6th century BCE, but Jains practising today are followers of Mahavira, the last of the twenty-four *Jinas*. *Jina* means 'conqueror', the one who has conquered inner enemies such as passion, attachment and aversion.

Mahavira was born in 599 BCE in the state of Bihar, India. His life followed a pattern somewhat similar to Gautama Buddha's (see p. 24), as he turned his back on a life of ease and luxury and set off in search of the ultimate Truth. His life is reflected in the name given to teachers of Jain, *Tirthamkara*, which means 'one who makes a ford' across the stream of existence.

Mahavira's influence was centred in the region of the Ganges, but during the 3rd century BCE it began to spread south and west. At that time a split occurred concerning the contents of the scriptures, and over the question of whether monks should or should not wear clothes. There is little practical divergence on these points of doctrine, but the schism remains to this day.

Svetamabaras 'white clad' monks wear white robes.
Digambaras 'sky clad' monks go totally unclothed as a symbol of their complete renunciation of the world.

Despite the split, Jain teachings have been conservatively maintained, though one of the very few changes is that worship in temples has been adopted. There are some beautiful temple complexes in western India, notably at Mount Abu and Palitana. Jain temples usually have a portal and colonnade, an open courtyard, and an inner shrine for the images. The principal image is flanked by two attendants and sometimes by many smaller images.

A Jain temple.

The Practice of Jainism

One of the laws of Jainism is to live without violence of any kind to living beings and Jains are strictly vegetarian in diet. In order to avoid crushing even an insect, some Jain monks and nuns wear masks over their mouths, strain their water before drinking, and sweep the path ahead of them as they walk. Farming was seldom practised by Jains, because of the danger of killing creatures in the soil; as a result, many Jains became traders. This was also a comparatively prosperous alternative to farming, and led to Jains gaining an influence in society that was disproportionate to their numbers.

Today Jainism is practised by some seven million people, mostly concentrated in India.

The Philosophy of Jainism

All actions, thoughts and deeds produce *karma*, which can be seen as a subtle material force capable of accumulation on a person's soul, weighing it down and condemning it to return to the world again. The *karma* produced by good actions dissipates easily, whereas that produced by bad actions clogs up the soul and can only be dispersed by the most extreme of ascetic practices. This severe austerity produces an energy called *tapas*, which means 'fire' or 'heat', and can be imagined as burning off the *karma* obstructing the soul. The most injurious *karma* is produced by the taking of life, no matter how small the creature, even unintentionally.

Once the soul, or *jiva,* is liberated, it rises to *nirvana,* the summit of the cosmos, where it dwells, blissful and unchanged. Total detachment and the absence of passion is also required to reach *nirvana;* Jains reach this by practising contemplation and meditation, and by rigorous self-discipline, such as fasting.

No appeal to a god is possible as, while Jains recognize a pantheon of gods, no one is worshipped as a saviour and Mahavira himself is venerated rather than worshipped.

Jainism Festivals

• The birthday of Lord Mahavira is celebrated with great enthusiasm and devotion. This generally falls in late March or early April (the 13th day of the month of *Chaitra* in the Indian calendar).

• The most important time of rejoicing in Jainism is held at Pasryushana, the season which begins the monsoon period. For eight days or longer, devout Jains fast and attend special services. At the close of the period of fasting, Jains ask forgiveness for past wrongs and promise to do good in future.

⇒ JUDAISM ⇐

> - Belief that the Jews are God's chosen people.
> - Holy book – the *Torah*.
> - 3500 year history.
> - Approximately 20 million followers.

Judaism, the oldest of the world's three great monotheistic religions, is the parent of Christianity and many other faiths.

Although they lived in a world noted for its multitude of gods, the Israelites were different in that they worshipped only one, so holy that his name could not be uttered. He had chosen the people of Israel to be a kingdom of priests and a holy nation, and in a solemn agreement known as the Covenant, the Israelites promised to obey God and fulfil His commandments. This covenant between God and the people is the foundation of the Jewish religion.

Torah scrolls: these are kept in the Ark (see p. 138) in the synagogue.

The Origins of Judaism

Judaism has its roots in the history of the Israelites which, according to the Bible, begins with God's exhortation to Abraham to settle in Canaan. His grandson Jacob had a vision in which God promised him many sons, who should possess the Land of Canaan. Jacob, or Israel as he became known, fathered twelve sons, from whom were descended the twelve tribes of Israel. The name Jew comes from Judah, the most powerful of these tribes.

Moses was the leader to whom God revealed His entire teaching, including the Ten Commandments; Moses received these laws on Mount Sinai around 1200 BCE. As a sign of reverence, Moses was instructed to build a sanctuary. The holiest area of the sanctuary contained a wooden chest overlaid with gold and in this chest – or Ark, as it became known – were two stone tablets upon which the ten commandments had been inscribed. The Ark of the Covenant was eventually placed in the temple built by Solomon in the 10th century BCE, in Jerusalem. The temple itself then became the central focus of worship as it was the only place where Jewish religious sacrifices could be carried out. With the ebb and flow of conquest in the region, the temple was destroyed and rebuilt several times until its final destruction by the Romans in CE 70.

After the final destruction of the temple and the crushing of the governing priesthood by the Romans, the *Torah* became the single unifying focus for the Jews, and the Rabbis (trained leaders of congregations or synagogues) took over the teaching function. The local synagogue became the meeting place for both worship and study.

Thus it was that the Romans' determination to stamp out the Jewish religion actually brought about its evolution into the Judaism of today, with its classical features of rabbinic scholarship and the fully formed synagogue worship. Study took the place of sacrifice as the central Jewish ritual, and the study of the ancient sacrificial rites came to seem almost equivalent to their performance.

Throughout history Jews have suffered varying degrees of persecution, culminating in the Holocaust at the hands of the Nazis during the Second World War. The justification for these atrocities is usually based on fear, suspicion born of ignorance, and distorted stereotypes which have grown up over the centuries. Judaism transcends ethnic boundaries, and despite absorbing local influences, Jewish communities wherever they live are united by the bond of their universal faith. They of course have the nationality of the country in which they live, but also assume a mantle of Jewishness with their personal practice and beliefs.

The shadow cast by the Holocaust made the founding of a Jewish homeland an event of the most profound significance, and Jews are deeply attracted to the modern state of Israel, which was founded in 1948.

Even before the Holocaust, Jews were often persecuted. The Wailing Wall is part of the Temple of Solomon, destroyed by the Babylonians.

Sacred Texts

The first five books of the *Old Testament,* the *Pentateuch,* tell the story of the Israelites from the time of Abraham, and set out God's ordinance as revealed to Moses and the Israelites. These same books form the *Torah,* which is central to Judaism.

The oral *Torah* is the collected rabbinic interpretations of the *Pentateuch.* The central text is the *Mishnah,* collected and edited in the 3rd century CE, which sets out the legal structure of Judaism. This in turn attracted commentary and interpretation, collected as the *Gemara.* There are two versions of the *Gemara:* the *Palestinian* and the *Babylonian.* Each, in association with the *Mishnah,* is called *Talmud.* The written *Torah* (which means 'teaching') refers to the *Pentateuch,* the first five books of the Hebrew Bible – *Genesis, Exodus, Leviticus, Numbers* and

Torah scroll with embroidered covering.

Deuteronomy – which, according to tradition, were revealed to Moses on Mount Sinai. The scroll of the *Torah* read publicly in the synagogue is hand-written and mounted on beautifully carved spindles. It rests on a lectern while being read, and there is usually a silver hand-shaped pointer so that it is not necessary to touch the page with one's fingers.

The Rabbis were the interpreters of the *Torah,* and their early interpretations were collected in the *Mishnah,* which deals with laws in six main areas covering agriculture, statutory feasts and festivals, the role of women, property and legal affairs, the temple and religious accoutrements and finally ritual purity. The *Mishnah,* with its attendant commentary the *Gemara,* comprises the *Talmud,* and is second only to the *Torah* in authority. The essence of the scholarly *Talmud* was distilled into the *Shulhan Aruch* which sets out basic guidelines for day-to-day life. The *Shulhan Aruch* was composed in the late 16th century CE, to re-present the legal structure in a more accessible form than the 3rd-century *Mishnah.*

Silver pointer for reading the Torah.

In *Deuteronomy,* chapter 6, Moses says, 'And these words, which I command thee this day, shall be in thine heart: And thou shalt bind them for a sign upon thine hand, and they shall be as frontlets between thine eyes.' These instructions are taken literally by Jewish tradition: observant Jews bind *Tefillin* (a pair of small, blackened, square cases), containing key texts from the *Torah,* to their arms and foreheads, and wear them for weekday morning prayers.

The Ten Commandments:

- To have no other gods but God.
- To make no idols.
- Not to misuse the name of God.
- To keep the sabbath holy.
- To honour one's parents.
- Not to commit murder.
- Not to commit adultery.
- Not to commit theft.
- Not to tell lies.
- Not to be covetous.

The Ten Commandments are often written above the Ark containing the Torah.

The Practice of Judaism

According to orthodox Jewish law a Jew is one born of a Jewish mother, although it is possible to become a Jew by conversion. The parents are responsible for religious education in the early years, but at school age the child attends religious classes which are held after school on weekdays and on Sunday mornings. There are lessons in the Hebrew language, the 3500-year history of the Jewish people, the customs for the many festivals, the food laws and all the teachings and stories in the Hebrew Bible. Girls have their *Bat Mitzvah* at twelve years and boys their *Bar Mitzvah* at thirteen. These are ceremonies, followed by great celebration, to denote that from this point on Jews are expected to be responsible for their actions and to fulfil all the duties of Judaism.

The most important time of the week is *Shabbat,* the Sabbath, which begins about half an hour before sunset on Friday. It recalls both the holiness of the seventh day of the creation and the deliverance of the people of Israel from Egypt. Its beginning is marked by the lighting of the *Shabbat* candles, usually by the woman of the household. The family shares a special meal, which starts with blessings over bread and wine. As *Shabbat* is a day of rest, Jews are not permitted to work: devout orthodox Jews do not use electrical appliances or cars, or undertake long journeys. *Havdalla* marks the end of *Shabbat* at nightfall on Saturday, when the family again gathers for blessings recited over wine, a box of sweet spices and a candle.

Jewish boy at his Bar Mitzvah.

Strict rules apply to both the kind of food which may be eaten and the way in which it is prepared. Food is called *kosher*, meaning 'permitted', when it is deemed fit to be eaten according to Jewish dietary laws. It is forbidden to prepare dairy products and meat together, or to serve them together at the same meal, so no butter for the bread or milk for the coffee if meat is on the menu. *Kosher* animals must have cloven hooves and chew the cud. *Kosher* fish must have fins and scales. *Kosher* birds are limited to domestic fowl. Animals and birds must be slaughtered in accordance with traditional practice. Strict observance of the laws also demands the use of separate sets of tableware for each type of food.

Devout Jews pray three times a day, morning, afternoon and evening. Men cover their head with a *kippa*, or skullcap, when they are at prayer. Some orthodox men wear a head covering throughout the day.

Lighting the Shabbat candles.

Jewish Movements

Like all major religions, Judaism has always had within it a number of movements, points of view and local emphases. These did not constitute sects, as such, historically, since rabbinic authority was universally accepted until the 18th century.

The Enlightenment in Europe challenged traditional philosophical and religious views and promoted new ideas on the nature of human beings, society and religion. For Jews, one result of this was a demand for reform in Judaism, particularly in Western Europe.

In Germany during the 1840s, **Reform Judaism** became institutionalized. This movement believed that because the Jews were no longer a nation, but citizens of the states where they lived, they were no longer bound by the whole religious code of law.

Reform Judaism was less successful in the rest of Europe, but it proved popular among the millions of Jewish immigrants to North America in the late 19th century. Today, Reform or Progressive Jews distinguish between aspects of Judaism that have eternal value, for example social idealism and the Sabbath, and matters such as gender distinction, which are seen as temporary and relative. For Progressive Jews, tradition must be revised and re-interpreted in the light of historical development and ritual takes second place to inner sincerity.

Conservative Judaism was founded in the 1840s. Although it did not adhere entirely to Orthodox standards, it clung more closely to historic Judaism, while making some concessions to the spirit of reform and the adaption of tradition to contemporary needs. It is a major force in the United States.

Reconstructionism was founded in the United States in the 1920s. Reconstructionists believe that Judaism is a religious civilization, and its religious elements are expressions of their specific culture. The movement rejects the notion of an all-knowing God who made a covenant with his chosen people, and does not believe that the Bible is the word of God, who is seen in non-personal terms, as a power guiding us toward salvation.

A pietistic movement called **Hasidism** began in 18th-century Poland and spread to Russia, Lithuania, Hungary and Palestine. Hasidism focused upon the spiritual and mystical aspects of Judaism in contrast to the emphasis on intellectual learning that was central to traditional Jewish societies. Hasidic leaders were believed to have special gifts from heaven beyond the abilities of ordinary rabbis. Today, Hasidic communities are particularly well-established in Israel and the United States.

The most traditional followers of rabbinic Judaism are commonly called **Orthodox,** those who uphold what they consider to be the unchanging faith of Israel. Orthodoxy affirms the authenticity of Biblical revelations and continues to grant full authority for Rabbinic law and interpretation. None of the major segments of modern Judaism have complete uniformity within it.

Rabbi at the festival of Rosh Hashana or New Year.

The Jewish Year

The Jewish calendar is lunar so the timing of festivals, according to the western Gregorian calendar, is rather flexible. The Jewish year begins with four festivals:

- **Rosh Hashana**

Jewish New Year and the believed anniversary of the creation of the world. This festival lasts for two days and marks the beginning of a ten-day period of penitence and reflection. The *Shofar* (ram's horn) is sounded in the synagogue on both of these days, as a call for renewed spiritual awareness.

- **Yom Kippur** (the Day of Atonement)

A day of fasting, repentance and spiritual renewal. It is the culmination of the Ten Days of Penitence.

- **Sukkot**, the Feast of the Tabernacles (or 'Booths')

This follows five days after Yom Kippur and is a week-long harvest festival to celebrate the forty-year journey of the Jews from Egypt to Israel. Many Jewish families build temporary huts ('tabernacles'), roofed with leaves and branches and have meals in them as a reminder of how their ancestors lived in the wilderness.

- **Simchat** *Torah*

This is the day after the harvest festival and is in celebration of the *Torah*. It marks the end of each year's reading of the complete *Torah* and the start of a new complete reading. The scrolls are paraded around the synagogue to the accompaniment of dancing and singing.

• Hanukkah

The Festival of Lights in November/December celebrates the winning back of the temple in Jerusalem 2000 years ago, its eight-day duration being symbolic of the miraculous story of how the supply of lamp oil lasted much longer than expected. The eight-branched candlestick *(menorah)* is also symbolic, with a new candle being lit on each of the eight days.

• Tu Bishevat

New Year for Trees is a one-day minor festival in January/ February when trees are planted and fruits from different trees are eaten in abundance.

- **Purim**

Held in February/March, the Carnival Festival celebrates the story of Esther, wife of the Persian King Xerxes, who defeated the plan of the King's steward, Haman, to destroy all the Jews in Persia 2500 years ago. The story of Esther is read in synagogues amidst joy and festivity.

- **Pesach**

The Passover, best known of all Jewish festivals, is celebrated around April and lasts for eight days. It recalls the escape of the Israelites from slavery in Egypt 3500 years ago, which is reflected in the recounting of the story of the Exodus

at a special family meal *(seder)* held in the home. Tradition has it that the departure from Egypt took place in such a hurry that there was no time to wait for the bread to rise as usual, and the Israelites took unleavened bread with them instead. Thus at Passover leavened bread is forbidden, and only unleavened *matzoh* may be eaten at this time.

- **Shavuot** (or Pentecost)

Celebrated in May/June, on the fiftieth day after the second day of Passover. The festival commemorates the giving of the *Torah* by God to Moses on Mount Sinai.

- **Tisha B'Av** (Fast of Av)

The religious year concludes in July/August with the solemn day-long fast which mourns the final destruction of the temple in Jerusalem in CE 70.

◀ *Recounting the story of Exodus at the Passover meal.*

Worship

The first temple in Jerusalem was built by Solomon in about 950 BCE, and lasted until 587 BCE when it was destroyed by the Babylonians. The second temple was built by Zarubbabel in 516 BCE. This modest structure was extended and embellished until its final and total destruction by the Romans in CE 70.

The Western (or Wailing) Wall.

The Western (or Wailing) Wall, a surviving portion of the original structure, is a point of pilgrimage and prayer. After the destruction of the temple, the synagogue became the principal place of Jewish communal worship.

Externally, synagogues tend to reflect local architectural custom rather than any constraints of Jewish tradition. The entrance gives access to a forecourt or vestibule which may provide washing facilities. Further doors lead to the main body of the synagogue.

An orthodox synagogue.

In orthodox synagogues, the sexes are separated, with a raised gallery or an area partitioned by a screen being provided for the women. The congregation is seated in the main body of the synagogue whilst the Rabbi will often sit facing the congregation. An annexe may accommodate a schoolroom and provide a focal point for communal activities.

Worshippers should face Jerusalem during prayer. The direction is indicated by the Ark, containing the sacred scroll *(Torah)* behind the Ark curtain *(Parochet)*. Services are led from a central raised dais *(Bimah)* where the covered desk for the reading of the *Torah* is located.

The Ark containing the Torah is kept behind a curtain.

Jewish Languages

Nowadays most of the world's 20 million Jews are descendants of the Ashkenazim, Jews from central and eastern Europe. The main Ashkenazic communities of the early Middle Ages were to be found in the Rhine basin where their language, Yiddish, evolved from a medieval German dialect and Hebrew. Around this language a rich culture in music, art and literature flourished. In Muslim-dominated Spain the Sephardic Jews (was taken to mean 'Spain') developed their own language, Ladino, a hybrid of Spanish and Hebrew, together with their own very distinctive intellectual and artistic culture.

- Hebrew is based on an alphabet of 22 consonants with separate vowel signs. It is written from right to left and generally the vowels are not shown.
- Hebrew is the language in which the Bible was first written, and is the living language of Israel today.

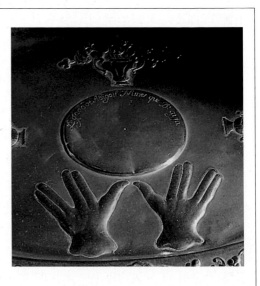

Jews are spread worldwide, this devotional symbol comes from South America.

RASTAFARI

- Founded in Jamaica during 1930s.
- 'Ras Tafari' refers to Haile Selassie I, Emperor of Ethiopia.
- Holy books – *Kebra Negast, Fetha Negast* and the Bible.
- 100,000 followers.

Rastafarians believe themselves to be the Chosen people, the Israelites of the Bible, redeemed with Ethiopia as the Promised Land. There are elements of Christianity in Rastafari, which arose in Jamaica, but instead of the European view, the emphasis is on African Black roots, with a repudiation of the White culture which tricked their African ancestors into enforced slavery. This view was held by many Jamaicans who, being descended from Africans, wished to link themselves with their homeland. It also allowed them to combine what they see as the true Christianity with African-Caribbean nationalism.

The Origins of Rastafari

Rastafari is a very young faith with an ancient tradition. It takes its name from that of the Ethiopian noble Lord Ras Tafari (Head Creator), Haile Selassie I ('Power of the Trinity'), King of kings, Lord of lords, conquering Lion of the Tribe of Judah, Emperor of Ethiopia, who traced His ancestry directly to the marriage of King Solomon and the Queen of Sheba. This is chronicled in the Bible: *Kings* 10: 4, 5 and 13, and is expanded in the *Kebra Negast* (Glory of the Kings), the ancient chronicle of Ethiopia.

On Ras Tafari's coronation on 2 November, 1930, Ethiopia, which had been a closed and hidden country, attracted the attention of the world. Its Emperor, together with the unique type of Christianity to be found in His country, found Himself a focus for many African-orientated revivalist movements. Most eminent among these was a young movement whose members' beliefs evolved within a quite distinct social context, during the misery of the Depression following European slavery in Jamaica and the rest of the Caribbean, and who, believing Emperor Haile Selassie I to be the true Messiah, called themselves Rastafari. Their ultimate aim was liberation and a millennial return to their ancestral home, Ethiopia. Ethiopia is cited as their ancient homeland. It is in the Bible: *Genesis* 2: 13.

Haile Selassie I, Emperor of Ethiopia (centre).

Haile Selassie I receiving a US Diplomat.

Today, however, Rastafarians place a greater emphasis on balancing self-help with their expectancy of the actual help of Emperor Haile Selassie I. Because He is not, as they describe it, 'readily visible' since 'rising' from the throne after the revolution in 1974, the faithful have had to look deeper into themselves to communicate with Him. They become more certain that, contrary to popular belief, He lives forever. Rastafarians maintain that Haile Selassie I is Almighty God, who is 'ever living'.

Festivals

- Emperor Haile Selassie I's birthday – 23 July
- His coronation – 2 November

Rastafarian Traditions

In Britain today, many within Rastafari have let go of a number of its original strictures, such as the requirement for a special diet, though all Rastafarians avoid pork and many are still *Ital* (vegetarians). Although not everyone in dreadlocks is Rastafari, all Rastafarians wear them; they also wear the colours of Ethiopia (green, gold and red). Rastafarians regard the smoking of marijuana as a mystical experience, to be used in worship. Rastafarian ideals include the desire for 'peace and love' and justice for all.

The most famous Rastafari symbol is that of the crowned Lion of Judah, carrying the Cross over one shoulder, and with an Ethiopian flag billowing around him.

The crowned Lion of Judah.

~ SHINTO ~

> - A major strand of Japanese religion, historically intertwined with Buddhism.
> - Focuses on local deities *(kami)*, shrines and communal festivals.
> - Transformed into a state-sponsored emperor-cult from 1868 to 1945.
> - Approximately 100 million followers worldwide, mainly in Japan.

The Origins of Shinto

Shinto (Chinese: *Shen tao*) means 'spirits' or 'gods' and the practices relating to them. This term was used in both China and Japan to distinguish the indigenous cults from Buddhist practices. In Japan, Shinto has traditionally meant practices relating to shrines *(jinja)*. Shrines are diverse sacred places marked by shrine buildings and associated with deities *(kami)*. Shrine rituals range from the private ceremonies of the imperial household at the most sacred Ise shrine, south-east of Kyoto, to innumerable local rites of agricultural fertility, purification and renewal.

Shinto until the 19th Century

During most of Japan's recorded history, from the 6th century CE to 1868, the shrines and their deities were understood within a Buddhist (see p. 23)/Confucian (see p. 78) world-view, originally introduced from China.

The Shinto religion is based around shrine worship.

> Buddhism provided Shinto with sacred written scriptures, personal morality and means of salvation, while Confucianism underpinned social ethics with ideas such as filial piety, purity and sincerity.

Local Shinto beliefs were relatively unsophisticated and many derived from Chinese Taoism (see p. 175). They developed alongside, and broadly supported, Buddhist and Confucian values.

In the Tokugawa period (CE 1600–1868) a Buddhist parish system was imposed nationwide, mainly to eradicate Catholicism, which had made substantial gains before Japan was closed to foreigners. The power of the

Offerings at a Shinto shrine.

Buddhist establishment provoked a reaction among Shinto shrine priests and Confucian scholars, who began a quest for evidence of a pre-Buddhist 'pure Japanese' religion. This scholarly pursuit, known as 'National Learning' *(kokugaku)* laid the foundation for a revival of Shinto later in the 19th century, when Japan once again opened her doors to the West.

> In 1868, the regime of the Tokugawa *shoguns* collapsed and an era of rapid European-style modernization and industrialization began, under the guise of the 'restoration' of ancient imperial rule. Buddhism was disestablished and a new form of Shinto, 'cleansed of Buddhist elements', was invented.

Shinto now preached devotion to the emperor at all costs, to the extent of laying down one's life for His sake.

By the 1890s, Shinto was officially named 'non-religious'; adherence to it was a civic duty rather than just a matter of personal belief. It was taught in schools and reinforced in standardized shrine rituals which revered the emperor as the descendant of the Sun Goddess, Amaterasu.

Modern Shinto

In the years up to 1945, the government resolutely enforced emperor worship, introducing it into other religions in Japan as well. Generations of modern Japanese grew up believing that modern, emperor-worshipping 'state Shinto' was the ancient, pure and indigenous religion of Japan. Nineteenth- and twentieth-century Shinto has therefore played a very significant role in the creation of the modern Japanese national consciousness.

In 1945, 'state Shinto' was disestablished by the Allied Occupation powers, real freedom of religion was enshrined in the new Constitution, and the emperor publicly renounced his claim to divinity.

Worshippers at the Minatogawa shrine in Kobe.

Shinto administrators regrouped in a voluntary national network of shrines which today constitutes Shinto, although there are numerous offshoots, sects and new religions which have connections with particular Shinto shrines and deities.

Festivals, Shrines and *Kami*

Communal festivals *(matsuri)* are now voluntary affairs; the largest ones can be spectacular. They feature magnificent floats decked with lanterns, a retinue of priests and other costumed participants, and one or more *mikoshi* (palanquins) for the *kami*. Many small local festivals retain the character of solemn religious rites followed by communal celebrations.

Shrine Worship

- There are about 100,000 registered shrines in Japan, many enshrining different *kami*.
- Shrines are marked by *torii*, distinctive large portals or uprights and crossbars, sometimes painted red.
- Within the shrine there is running water for visitors to rinse and purify their hands and mouths before approaching the *kami*.
- Large shrines have various other gates, bridges or fences to cross as one approaches the most sacred space, the residence of the *kami*.
- Ordinary worship consists of a small cash offering, hand-clapping and silent petition.

It is popularly believed that there are 80 million *kami* in Japan, but among the 100,000 or so shrines, a few eminent *kami*, such as Inari, Kompira, Hachiman and Tenjin, predominate. Each of these great *kami* has many thousands of 'branch' shrines throughout the country. Shrines are known mainly for the special benefits they offer such as business prosperity, exam success or good luck in marriage. The upkeep of the local shrine depends on contributions from the local community, and, especially in the case of large shrines, on donations from those who visit, to buy amulets and seek benefits through a ritual.

Shrine Priests

Shrine priests visit local businesses, construction sites and newly completed buildings to perform purifying rituals for each new phase of a project. Babies are normally brought to the shrine about a month after they are born, and young children visit periodically for the *shichi-go-san* (ages 3, 5 and 7) rites. Since the early 1900s, Japanese weddings have normally been conducted by Shinto priests. However, with the exception of the war-dead, who are enshrined in the great Yasukuni Jinja in Tokyo, matters of death, salvation and the afterlife are dealt with almost exclusively by Buddhist priests at Buddhist temples.

This shrine is for the spirits of dead babies and children.

Although shrines were 'cleansed' of Buddhist connections in 1868,
Buddhism and Shinto are not separate in the minds of Japanese people,
and most visitors to Shinto shrines are therefore also Buddhists.

Despite the upheavals of the late 19th century, Buddhism and Shinto
remain intertwined in Japanese life.

Ritual dance of the Shrine Priests. ▲

~ SIKHISM ~

- First Sikh Guru – Nanak, born CE 1469.
- Belief in one God.
- Holy book – the *Guru Granth Sahib*.
- Approximately 20 million followers.

The Sikh community is referred to as the *Guru Panth* and spiritual guidance is provided by the holy scriptures of the *Guru Granth Sahib*.

Nanak, the first Guru, and founder of Sikhism.

The Origins of Sikhism

The Ten Gurus

The founder of Sikhism and its first Guru was Nanak (a Guru is a religious leader giving spiritual guidance to his disciples). Nanak was born in CE 1469 to a Hindu family in the Punjab, which was then under Muslim rule. Nanak's early years were therefore influenced by a background of both Hindu (see p. 85) and Muslim (see p. 106) teachings; however he soon became disillusioned with the intolerance shown by the leaders of both these major faiths.

When he was about thirty years old, Nanak preached his first sermon in which he proclaimed 'there is neither Hindu nor Muslim'; that is to say, God is not interested in our religious labels, but in the way in which we conduct ourselves. All religions, he taught, were ways to the same one God, and all should be respected.

The Guru travelled widely to places as far apart as Tibet in the north, Sri Lanka in the south and Baghdad in the west, spreading his message of tolerance, equality of all human beings, and care and compassion for the disadvantaged. He emphasized the complete equality of women in both worship and secular life.

Angad, whom Nanak had nominated as the second Guru, collected Nanak's poems and hymns, thus establishing what were to become the principal Sikh scriptures. The first authoritative version of the scriptures, the *Adi Granth,* was completed by the fifth Guru, Arjun, who led the community from CE 1581. It was Arjun who built the original Harimandir, the Golden Temple at Amritsar.

The new prosperity and increasingly high profile of the community under Arjun's leadership led to conflict with the Mogul emperor Jehangir, on whose orders Arjun was captured and imprisoned in Lahore. After being

The Ten Gurus.

subjected to horrific torture with hot sand he died from his injuries in 1606.

Arjun's son Har Gobind succeeded as the sixth Guru, and under his leadership Sikhs took the first steps to actively defend themselves when increased Mogul pressure forced a retreat into the Himalayan foothills. The stand-off between Moguls and Sikhs continued until the ninth Guru, Tegh Bahadur, true to Guru Nanak's teachings of tolerance, roused the Mogul emperor to new fury by defending the right of Hindus to worship in the manner of their choice. He was tortured and died a martyr in 1675.

The tenth and last Guru, Tegh Bahadur's nine-year-old son Gobind Singh, grew to be a renowned warrior and, focusing on his father's martyrdom, he welded the Sikhs into a distinctive and militarily effective community prepared to defend their egalitarian teachings as well as the rights of others. Founded in 1699 at Ananpur, it became known as the *Khalsa,* the community of 'pure ones'. Under his stewardship, the hymns and poems of Tegh Bahadur were added to the *Adi Granth* and instead of appointing a human successor he decreed that the scriptures should become the community's final teacher, the *Guru Granth.*

Guru Nanak, the founder of Sikhism

Sacred Texts

The *Guru Granth Sahib,* the holy book of Sikhism, contains hymns written by the Gurus as well as hymns by Hindu and Muslim writers, and provides the teaching and guidance no longer available from a human Guru. It is also called the *Adi Granth* ('first book') and is regarded as the final Sikh Guru. The *Guru Granth Sahib* is written in the Gurmukhi language, and is treated with as much reverence as if it were indeed a human Guru. In a temple or a private house, it is kept in a special room of its own. It rests on a quilt and cushions on a small table called the *Manji Sahib,* and is protected by a canopy called a *chanani,* and by special cloths wrapped round it called *rumala.*

Sikh reading the Guru Granth Sahib.

Sikh Beliefs and Doctrine

The Sikh teaching of monotheism is based on the concept of God not belonging to any particular faith. Belief in the one God transcends the barriers between religions. Images of God are considered meaningless since God cannot be represented in human or physical form, and can only be experienced through meditation, worship and selfless service to others.

One distinctive feature is the importance of the concept of the Guru. This can be God himself, as the ultimate teacher, whose words and thoughts were communicated to mankind through the ten living Gurus. Belief in the equality of all men and women is manifested in the *langar,* the communal meal served after a service, to which all are welcomed, Sikhs and non-Sikhs alike. The origins of this lie in the reaction to, and rejection of, the caste system.

The religion has no trained priesthood: anyone can lead the service, although there are individuals specially trained to read the Gurmukhi script in which the *Guru Granth* is written. Sikhs believe in reincarnation even to the extent that in previous lives they may have lived in other life forms, but it is only the human incarnation that can experience the love of God. Death is therefore perceived as the next stage in a succession of lives in much the same way as going to sleep at night. In fact one of the principal funeral prayers, the *Sohila Mahala,* is said before going to bed.

Sikhs are forbidden tobacco, alcohol, drugs unless medicinal, and the eating of meat slaughtered by bleeding to death, since it is considered cruel to animals. They must also refrain from gambling, stealing and adultery. Charity and community service are actively encouraged. All Sikh men have the surname Singh (lion) and all Sikh women, the surname Kaur (princess).

Worship and Traditions

Sikhs usually worship together at a *gurdwara,* which means 'door of the guru'. *Gurdwaras* vary greatly in shape, size and appearance, with the best-known and most holy being the Golden Temple at Amritsar in the Punjab. This is surrounded by water and is approached via a causeway. Gurdwaras are normally purpose-built, but outside India Sikh communities have converted existing buildings. Whatever the building's appearance, all *gurdwaras* share some common features.

There is a room for worship, and there is also a kitchen, where the *langar,* a free meal for all, is prepared, and a room in which it is eaten. There is usually a classroom in which children are taught the *Gurmukhi.*

The Golden Temple at Amritsar.

The Brotherhood of Sikhs is called the *Khalsa*. Sikh men must wear the five symbols of their faith, the Five Ks, so called for their initial letter in Punjabi:

- *kesh* – uncut hair and beard.
- *kangha* – comb to groom and fix the hair in place in the turban.
- *kara* – circular steel wristband.
- *kirpan* – miniature sword (this and the *kara* both remind Sikhs of their responsibilities).
- *kach* – knee-length shorts.

Khalsa Sikh.

Festivals

Some major Sikh festivals are held on the same day as Hindu festivals, such as Holi and Diwali (see pp. 103–104). However, for Sikhs they have a different meaning, commemorating special events in the lives of the Gurus. In addition, Sikhs also celebrate festivals called *gurpurbs*. During these the *Guru Granth Sahib* is often read from beginning to end, and may be carried through the streets in procession.

Sikh boys in a festival procession.

The Sikh Community Today

After the collapse of the Mogul empire in the mid-18th century, the Sikhs established dominance in the Punjab until their army was defeated at the hands of the British in 1846 and 1849. Their fighting skills were so admired that Sikhs were recruited by the British army, and many gave their lives in the two World Wars.

The 20th century has seen continued strife for Sikhs in the Punjab, both with the colonial British and later with Muslims and Hindus. The partition of the Indian sub-continent in 1947 split the Punjab between Muslim Pakistan and Hindu India. Sikhs opted to join India, but there has been a growing sense of betrayal, particularly after the Indian army attacked the Golden Temple in 1984. Many now feel that an independent state is the only safeguard from Hindu extremism.

Many Sikhs now live outside their native Punjab, the main exodus occurring after 1947. The majority came to Britain although some settled in Canada, the United States and South and East Africa. Communities try to maintain their culture and traditions through educational and social activities.

A Sikh wedding.

TAOISM

- Key teacher – Lao Tzu.
- Holy book – *Tao Te Ching*.
- Approximately 20 million followers worldwide.

The *Tao* is the Way, the ineffable unchanging essence and principle of everything in heaven and on earth. This metaphysical absolute produces and sustains all things, but without intent or struggle. To accord with the Way one must be without desires, intentions or volitions.

'There is nothing right or wrong, but thinking makes it so,' said William Shakespeare in a later age. The quest of Tao aims to go beyond the human constructs of good and bad, or sickness and health, and to achieve serenity.

The Origins of Taoism

Taoism is a philosophical and religious tradition centred on the Tao. It had its first expression in the works of a number of philosophers during the 6th and 4th centuries BCE. Among these works is a famous collection called *Tao Te Ching,* which is traditionally attributed to Lao Tzu, a shadowy figure believed to have lived in China in about 500 BCE. Lao Tzu is the father of Tao philosophy and is now treated as the supreme deity. He is believed to have been a keeper of the imperial archives at Luoyang in the Chinese province of Henan in the 6th century BCE. According to ancient legend, just before he withdrew from the world he was persuaded by a gatekeeper to write down his teachings for posterity. The essence of Taoism is contained in the 81 chapters of *Tao Te Ching,* which have provided one of the major influences on Chinese thought and culture over the last 2500 years.

Statue at Luoyang in China, where Lao Tzu is believed to have been keeper of the imperial archives.

In the 2nd century CE, Taoist thought and themes developed into their second stage, and religious movements and organizations, which aimed at gaining immortality, emerged as the cult of the Tao. The first of such organizations was established by a certain Chang Tao-ling who in CE 142, after dreaming of Lao Tzu, took the title T'ien-shih ('heavenly master'). He set up a new scheme of worship in which the adherents were required to contribute five pecks of rice to the movement. As a result, this came to be known as 'The Way of Five Pecks of Rice'.

The opening lines of Lao Tzu's *Tao Te Ching:*
'The Tao that can be spoken is not the eternal Tao;
The name that can be named is not the unchanging name;
The nameless is called the beginning of heaven and earth;
The named is the mother of all things.'

Although there are many different sects of Taoist religion, their followers are characterized by their seeking of freedom (freedom from mortality, from political constraints, and from separation from the Tao) and their only differences are in the ways in which they seek to attain this freedom. Over the years they have often been at odds with government. Yet in relation to Confucianism (see p. 78), Taoism has established itself as the other side of the Chinese culture and tradition, and the typical Taoist ideas such as the *Yin* and *Yang,* the five elements and Tai Ch'i (the Great Ultimate, a series of 108 complex slow movements) have become an inseparable part of the world-view of the Chinese, as well as of many other nations.

Taoism in Relation to other Chinese Faiths

- The teachings of Taoism overlap with Chinese Buddhism.
- Taoism is more spiritual than Confucianism.

B uddhism (see p. 23) contributed to the Taoist religion, influencing it to arrange its scriptures in imitation of Buddhist models, and to establish monasteries, but the two religions were always somewhat in competition, not only for souls but also for Chinese Imperial patronage. Taoism was less affected by Confucianism (see p. 78), as the latter is influenced more by day-to-day rules of conduct, whereas Taoism is concerned with a more spiritual level of existence. However it should be noted that the various religions of China have co-existed with greater harmony than those of most other countries and, despite this century's political vicissitudes, Taoist philosophy and religion survive both in China and abroad.

Taoist Hanging Temple.

Taoist Practices

Taoist understanding works in harmony with life's circumstances and respects the inner nature of all things. This cultivation of serenity and the understanding of (and ability to live at ease with) the natural balance produced by universal laws can be developed by meditation and by the use of breathing techniques. However the first step towards understanding the Tao is to think and act spontaneously, without effort.

'In the pursuit of learning, every day something is acquired.
In the pursuit of Tao, every day something is discarded.
The world is ruled by letting things take their course.
It cannot be ruled by interfering.'
Lao-Tzu, *Tao Te Ching*

Taoist priest – Taoist teaching encourages an understanding of the natural balance and harmony of all things.

ZOROASTRIANISM

- Zoroaster, born in Persia between 1200 and 600 BCE.
- Holy Book – the *Avesta*.
- Approximately 200,000 followers.

Zoroastrianism is the religion of the followers of the ancient Persian prophet Zoroaster (whose name comes from the Greek rendering of the name Zarathustra), who is believed to have been born between 1200 and 600 BCE. The precise dating is difficult to establish, because of a lack of historical sources, but linguistic analysis of religious texts favours the earlier date.

The Origins of Zoroastrianism

The Life of Zoroaster

Zoroaster was born into a community of settled farmers, and became a priest in the religion of the time, one which had an imagery drawn from nature and a pantheon based on natural forces. He married and had several children. At around the age of 30 he had a series of visions which convinced him of the truth of the new doctrine he had been formulating.

His teachings were a threat to the established ways, in particular because of his opposition to such features as sacrifice and the use of hallucinogenics in ritual. This led to opposition from the other priests and ultimately to his assassination, possibly by a priest. During his life, however, Zoroaster managed to convert King Vishtasp, ruler of asmall neighbouring kingdom, and from these small beginnings the religion spread and grew until it had become the acknowledged religion of the mighty Persian empire established by the Achaemenians in the 6th century BCE.

Zoroastrian fire temple.

The Spread of Zoroastrianism

Zoroastrianism remained the state religion of the Persian empire from about 600 BCE to CE 650, when Persia, and Zoroastrianism with it, was overrun by the Arabs and the forces of Islam. Thus for 1000 years it was considered by many to be the most influential religion in the known civilized world. The invading Muslims persecuted the Zoroastrians, compelling them to convert or retreat, but in the remote districts, and at the far edges of Iran, worshippers clung to their faith, calling themselves *Mazdayasnians,* 'worshippers of god'.

At some time in the 10th century CE a group of Zoroastrians seeking to escape the oppression prevalent in Iran settled in North-west India, where they have become known as Parsees, 'Persians', and have achieved great distinction.

Finally, in the 19th century, official tolerance was decreed within Iran, though in practice Muslim persecution of Zoroastrians persisted well into the 20th century. Since 1979, when the Islamic Revolution in Iran took place, a significant diaspora of Iranian Zoroastrians has been established, mainly in Canada and California.

Although today there are fewer Iranian Zoroastrians than Parsees, the Parsee population is in decline, whereas the population of Iranian Zoroastrians continues to rise.

Zoroastrian worship focuses on fire, the symbol of purity.

Holy Texts

Zoroaster's utterances have been preserved in the *Gathas,* a series of hymns which are the only contemporary source of information on Zoroaster. The *Gathas,* together with other texts, were collected to form the *Avesta,* the holy book of the Zoroastrians. According to Zoroastrian tradition, the texts have been completely destroyed twice, once by Alexander the Great and once by the Arabs. They survived only through the oral form until they were finally noted down in the late 18th century by a French philologist, Anquetil du Perron. The texts are difficult and obscure, and therefore open to varied interpretation, but they show Zoroaster to have been a mystic and prophet, a poet and a profound thinker. His coherent, careful thought may have led him to his doctrine, but it was his visions which convinced him of the truth.

Remote fire temple on a hillside in Iran.

The Practice of Zoroastrianism

The teachings of Zoroaster centre on a god of complete goodness, Ahura Mazda ('Wise Lord'), who created the world and who is wholly beneficent. In opposition to his creation of the Good Spirit (Spenta Mainyu) there stands his absolute opposite, Angra Mainyu ('Destructive Spirit'), the embodiment of evil. Thus Zoroastrianism is one of the earliest monotheistic religions, though encompassing an ethical dualism. The central tenet is of free will and of personal responsibility in making the right choice between good and evil. The good reap the rewards of personal happiness in this life and ultimately go to heaven, while the evil are condemned to hell.

Zoroastrians are highly optimistic, certain that good will prevail, and are determined to partake of this good through the highest moral ideals, and in the fight against evil in all its forms during their life on earth.

Towers of Silence, where followers of Zoroaster traditionally disposed of their dead.

The role of priest *(dastur/mobed)* is hereditary and has been maintained through priestly families who are the traditional repositories of religious knowledge. At initiation (*sedreh pushi* or *navjote*), Zoroastrians put on a sacred cord *(koshti)* and a white shirt *(sedreh)*, to remind them of the battle they must fight against evil.

The followers of Zoroaster traditionally disposed of their dead by exposing their corpses to birds and animals in special buildings known as Towers of Silence. Today this practice has died out everywhere apart from India, where it is declining rapidly.

Zoroastrian Symbols

- Zoroastrians tend not to have images, statues or temples. Worship of God, Ahura Mazda, focuses on fire, the symbol of purity.
- The Zoroastrian religious symbol is a wide-winged bird known as *fravahar*. It is depicted on the ruins at Persepolis, hovering over the Achaemenid monarchs. It is thought to represent the *farr*, or presence of the divine wisdom of Ahura Mazda, Wise Lord.

Zoroastrians worship their god, Ahura Mazda, in the form of fire.

The Influence of Zoroastrianism

Zoroastrianism has had an immense influence on other religions, especially Islam (see p. 106), Judaism (see p. 137) and Christianity (see p. 39), foreshadowing their belief in final judgement, heaven, hell, the resurrection and a saviour. Zoroaster has been identified with various *Old Testament* figures, including Nimrod and Ezekiel.

The best known Zoroastrian priests (known as *mogh* or *magi*) were the wise men of the East, who have become famous because they followed the star to Bethlehem, and brought gifts to the baby Jesus Christ (see p.40).

The best known followers of Zoroastrianism were the wise men of the East, or the Magi, who came to worship the Christ child at Bethlehem.

Expert Authenticators and Contributors

FOR THE ORIGINAL EDITION

General Consultant – Elizabeth Breuilly has written extensively on religion for an educational and general readership. As a member of ICOREC (the International Consultancy on Religion, Education and Culture) she has also worked with agencies in Kenya and Tanzania encouraging multi-faith responses to current developments in education and conservation, and has contributed to numerous texts on religious issues, ecology and mythology.

Overall Authenticator – Robert Vint has organized interfaith dialogues and lectures, by leaders and representatives of the major faiths, for the last eight years. He founded and currently administers REEP (the Religious Education and Environment Programme) – a teacher training organization. Robert also lectures on the environmental teachings of the world's religions.

Bahá'í Faith – The Hon. Barney Leith has been a Bahá'í for over 30 years and is a member of the national governing council of the UK Bahá'í community. He is an international speaker on the Bahá'í Faith, has broadcast on BBC national and World Service radio, and leads workshops in Europe and the United States on the Bahá'í teachings and community life.

Buddhism – Stephen Batchelor is a former Buddhist monk, a writer and a translator of Buddhist books. He is also the Director of Studies of the Sharpham College, Devon, England.

Christianity – Alan Brown, a practising Christian, is Director of The National Society's Kensington R.E. Centre and R.E. (Schools) Officer of the General Synod Board of Education. He has written a great many books about the Christian faith and world religions, as well as numerous articles, reviews and booklets. He is also a tutor and examiner for The Open University course, 'The Religious Quest'.

Christianity – Sister Victoria Hummell, B. Phil. (ED), MA, is a member of the Sisters of the Assumption, a broadly educational Roman Catholic order. She has studied Theology and R.E. in Ireland and England and is currently R.E. Advisor for the Diocese of Westminster. She is an Ofsted inspector and trainer of denominational inspectors, and a member of the executive of the National Board of R.E. Advisors and Inspectors (NBRAI).

Confucianism and Taoism – Dr Yao is a specialist in Chinese philosophy and religions, and has been teaching courses on Confucianism, Taoism, Chinese Buddhism and comparative ethics for many years. Among his recent publications is *Confucianism and Christianity: A Comparative Study of Jen and Agape*. Dr Yao is the Director of Religion, Ethics & Society at the University of Wales, Lampeter.

Hinduism – Dilip Kadodwala is a practising Hindu. Dilip is an Inspector for Leicester County Council and an Advisor on Religious Education for the council.

Islam – Umar Hegedüs is a practising Muslim and works with The Islamic Consultancy and Information Service (ICIS), a key agency in advising and working with schools, colleges and universities, LEAs, Health Authorities, Employers and Government Departments. ICIS works with writers, radio and television programme makers and publishers to ensure future books, programmes and articles about Islam, or referring to Islamic topics, are free of errors.

Jainism – Dr Vinod Kapashi is a practising Jain and President of the Jain council in England.

Judaism – Jonathan Gorsky is Education Officer of the Council of Christians and Jews, and editor of Common Ground, the C. C. J. journal. A practising Jew, he is former Education Director of Yakar, a well-known Jewish cultural foundation, and contributes regularly to religious journals on matters connected with Christian-Jewish relations.

Rastafari – Ras Kwende B. Anbessa-Ebanks, a practising Rastafarian, is an executive secretary and chaplain with the Ethiopian World Federation. He is also the author of several books on Rastafarianism.

Shinto – Dr Brian Bocking is Professor and Head of the Study of Religions Dept. at Bath College of Higher Education, he is also President of the British Association for the Study of Religions. Previously he taught at the University of Stirling, Scotland and the University of Tsukuba, Japan. His publications include *Nagarjuna in China*, (Edwin Mellen Press, 1995) and *A Popular Dictionary of Shinto*, (Curzon Press, 1996).

Sikhism – Indarjit Singh, JP, OBE is a practising Sikh and Chairman of the Sikh Council for Interfaith Religions in Britain. He is a journalist and broadcaster, Editor of the *Sikh Messenger* and a frequent contributor to *The Times*, *Guardian* and *Independent*.

Zoroastrianism – Shahin Bekhradnia is a postgraduate researcher of Anthropology, based at St Anthony's College, Oxford. She is the author of many lectures and several publications and her research takes her regularly to Tajikistan in the former Soviet Union. A practising Zoroastrian, Ms Bekhradnia is active in inter-faith movements and a teacher of Ancient History.

Illustration Notes

5 Bodhisattva. Courtesy of Christie's Images. **7** Death Mask of the Pharaoh Tutankhamen. Courtesy of AKG. **8** The Death God Anubis Leans Over the Body of Sennutem. Courtesy of AKG. **9** Maya Deities Represented on Vase from Chama. Courtesy of Mary Evans Picture Library. **10** Aztec God Xipe Tolec. Courtesy of MacQuitty International Collection. **11** The Parthenon in Athens. Courtesy of AKG. **12** Hadrian's Wall. Courtesy of MacQuitty International Collection. **14-5** The Ride of the Valkyries by Karl Engel. Courtesy of Christie's Images. **16** Tanderagee Stone Figure. Courtesy of Visual Arts Library. **17** Tomb of the Báb. Courtesy of Martin Palmer/Circa Photo Library. **19** Bahá'ís on Pilgrimage Enter the Shrine of the Báb to Pray. Courtesy of the Bahá'í Publishing Trust. **20** Bahá'í Temple, Chicago. Courtesy of the Bahá'í World Centre. **21** Universal Seat of Justice, Mount Carmel. Courtesy of the Bahá'í World Centre. **22** Abdu'l-Bahá. Courtesy of the Bahá'í World Centre. **23** Gautama Buddha. Courtesy of Twin Studio/Circa Photo Library. **24** The Birth of the Buddha. Courtesy of AKG. **25** Buddha Meditating by a Waterfall by Li Ruiqing. Courtesy of Christie's Images. **27** The Six Stages of Reincarnation. Courtesy of AKG. **28** Buddhist Pali Scriptures. Courtesy of Martin Palmer/Circa Photo Library. **29** Buddhist Saffron Robes. Courtesy of Martin Palmer/Circa Photo Library. **31** Reclining Buddha, Sri Lanka. Courtesy of Martin Palmer/Circa Photo Library. **33** Statue of Kuan Yin, Bodhisattva of Mercy. Courtesy of John Smith/Circa Photo Library. **34** Bodhidharma. Courtesy of John Smith/Circa Photo Library. **35** Shadakshari Avalokitesvara. Courtesy of AKG. **37** Footprints of the Buddha. Courtesy of MacQuitty International Collection. **39** The Lamentation with Two Male Saints by Benozzo Gozzoli. Courtesy of Christie's Images. **40** The Nativity, St Giles, Edinburgh. Courtesy of MacQuitty International Collection. **41** A Tryptich: Christ Before Pilate by Antonio Vazquez. Courtesy of Christie's Images. **42** The Crucifixion with Two Prophets. Courtesy of Christie's Images. **43** Christ Washing the Disciples' Feet by the School of Arezzo. Courtesy of Christie's Images. **44** The Apostles Peter and Paul by Bartolomeo Vivarini. Courtesy of AKG. **46** Cross and Chi Rho Symbol. Courtesy of John Smith/Circa Photo Library. **47** (t) Jerusalem from the Mount of Olives. Courtesy of Travel Photo International; (b) St Peter's, Rome. Courtesy of Travel Photo International. **48** John Calvin. Courtesy of AKG. **50** The Trinity by Master of the Vitae Imperatorum. Courtesy of Christie's Images. **52** (t) Priest at Mass. Courtesy of John Smith/Circa Photo Library; (b) Baptism. Courtesy of John Smith/Circa Photo Library. **54** Latin Bible. Courtesy of John Smith/Circa Photo Library. **55** Book of Hours: Joachim and Anna at the Golden Gate. Courtesy of Christie's Images. **56** St Paul's Cathedral. Courtesy of AKG. **58** (t) Good Friday Procession. Courtesy of John Smith/Circa Photo Library; (b) Easter/Baptism Candle. Courtesy of John Smith/Circa Photo Library. **59** Virgin Mary and Child, Syrian Orthodox. Courtesy of Martin Palmer/Circa Photo Library. **60** Jesus and Mother of God, Orthodox Bible. Courtesy of John Smith/Circa Photo Library. **61** Pope. Courtesy of Apostolic Annunciation. **62** Virgin Mary, Roman Catholic. Courtesy of John Fryer/Circa Photo Library. **63** Back of a Chasuble of Rare Green Velvet. Courtesy of Christie's Images. **64** Book of Common Prayer. Courtesy of John Smith/Circa Photo Library. **65** Madonna and Child in a Mandorla. Courtesy of Christie's Images. **67** Martin Luther. Courtesy of AKG. **70** Salvation Army and Good Friday Procession. Courtesy of John Smith/Circa Photo Library. **71** Pentecost — Large Historiated Initial D. Courtesy of Christie's Images. **73** (t) Mormon Tabernacle Choir. Courtesy of MacQuitty International Collection; (b) Mormon Temple in Salt Lake City. Courtesy of AKG. **75** Chinese Church. Courtesy of Tjaling Halbertsma/Circa Photo Library. **79** Confucian Disciple Outside Tomb of Confucius. Courtesy of Martin Palmer/Circa Photo Library. **81** Confucius. Courtesy of Visual Arts Library. **83** Qi Lin from the House of Confucius. Courtesy of Martin Palmer/Circa Photo Library. **86** Vishnu and Escorts. Courtesy of John Smith/Circa Photo Library. **88** Illustration to the Mahabharata by Jaipur. Courtesy of Christie's Images. **89** Sadhu Delhi. Courtesy of MacQuitty International Collection. **90-1** Rama and Sita. Courtesy of John Smith/Circa Photo Library. **93** Incarnations of Vishnu. Courtesy of John Smith/Circa Photo Library. **94** (t) Hindu Temple, Delhi. Courtesy of Martin Palmer/Circa Photo Library; (b) Hindus Undergo their Washing Ritual. Courtesy of AKG. **95** Shiv Mandir Temple, Varansi. Courtesy of Bipinchandra J. Mistry/Circa Photo Library. **96** Ganesha. Courtesy of John Smith/Circa Photo Library. **97** Shiva Dancing in a Circle of Flames. Courtesy of Bipinchandra J. Mistry/Circa Photo Library. **98** (l) Man Dressed as Hanuman. Courtesy of William Holtby/Circa Photo Library; (r) The Goddess Kali. Courtesy of Bipinchandra J. Mistry/Circa Photo Library. **100** Brahmin Practising Yoga. Courtesy of Bipinchandra J. Mistry/Circa Photo Library. **102** (t) Krishna Devotees in Temple. Courtesy of John Smith/Circa Photo Library; (b) Hare Krishna, Washington DC. Courtesy of MacQuitty International Collection. **104** Arti Offered at Diwali. Courtesy of John Smith/Circa Photo Library. **105** Pilgrims at Holi. Courtesy of Robyn Beeche/Circa Photo Library. **107** Mughal Illuminated Prayer Book. Courtesy of Jak Kilby. **109** The Ka'bah Makkah During Prayer. Courtesy of Jak Kilby. **110** Qur'an. Courtesy of Visual Arts Library. **111** The Prophet's Mosque, Minarets at Dusk. Courtesy of Jak Kilby. **112** Illustrated Page, Depiction of the Ka'bah. Courtesy of Robyn Beeche/Circa Photo Library. **113** 'Allah' — Brass Plate on the Dome of the Rock, Jerusalem. Courtesy of Jak Kilby. **114** 'Ali' — Medallion on the Interior Wall of Al-Aqsa Mosque, Jerusalem. Courtesy of Jak Kilby. **115** Imam and Congregation in Prayer. Courtesy of John Smith/Circa Photo Library. **116** Qur'an. Courtesy of Visual Arts Library. **117** Selim Teaching His Son Omar the Qur'an. Courtesy of Jak Kilby. **118** (t) Qur'an. Courtesy of Ged Murray/Circa Photo Library; (b) The Whole World is a Mosque. Courtesy of Jak Kilby. **119** Dome of the Rock, Jerusalem. Courtesy of Travel Photo International. **120** Qur'an. Courtesy of Visual Arts Library. **122** Hussein in Ihram, Ready for Pilgrimage. Courtesy of Jak Kilby. **123** Prayer Outside Regent's Park Mosque. Courtesy of John Smith/Circa Photo Library. **126** Negri Sembilan State Mosque, Seremban, Malaysia. Courtesy of Jak Kilby. **127** Detail of the Mihrab, Hasssan Mosque, Cairo. Courtesy of Jak Kilby. **128** Mosque of Suleiman the Magnificent, Istanbul. Courtesy of Travel Photo International. **129** (t) Traditional Qur'anic School, Sudan. Courtesy of Jak Kilby; (b) Al-Aqsa Mosque — Interior Looking South. Courtesy of Jak Kilby. **130** Islamia School Science Class. Courtesy of Jak Kilby. **131** Shoe Rack at the Prophet's Mosque. Courtesy of Jak Kilby. **132** Bhagavan Mahavira's Last Sermon, from the Illustrated Bhagavan Mahavira. Courtesy of Dr Vinod Kapashi. **134** Jain Temple, Khajuraho. Courtesy of Travel Photo International. **137** Torah Scrolls in the Ark. Courtesy of Barrie Searle/Circa Photo Library. **139** Hassidic Jews, Western Wall. Courtesy of Zbigniew Kösc/Circa Photo Library. **140** Torah Scrolls. Courtesy of Michael Edwards/Circa Photo Library. **141** Torah-Finger. Courtesy of AKG. **142** Ten Commandments in Synagogue Above Ark. Courtesy of Barrie Searle/Circa Photo Library. **143** Bar Mitzvah, Western Wall. Courtesy of Barrie Searle/Circa Photo Library. **144** Mother and Daughter Bringing in the Sabbath. Courtesy of Barrie Searle/Circa Photo Library. **146** Rabbi at Rosh Hashana Festival. Courtesy of Ged Murray/Circa Photo Library. **148–9** Passover — Haggadah. Courtesy of Barrie Searle/Circa Photo Library. **150** (t) Prayer at the Western Wall. Courtesy of William Holtby/Circa Photo Library; (b) Orthodox Synagogue, Manchester. Courtesy of John Smith/Circa Photo Library. **151** Cover of Ark with Menorah Embroidery. Courtesy of Barrie Searle/Circa Photo Library. **152** (t) Mezuzah. Courtesy of Circa Photo Library; (b) Willemsbid Synagogue. Courtesy of MacQuitty International Collection. **154** Emperor Haile Selassi. Courtesy of Barnaby's Picture Library. **155** Emperor Haile Selassie Receives US Diplomat Outside Palace in Adis Ababa, Ethiopia. Courtesy of Barnaby's Picture Library. **156** Crowned Lion of Judah. Courtesy of Ras Kwende B. Anbessa-Ebanks. **158** Shinto Shrine. Courtesy of Joanne O'Brien/Circa Photo Library. **159** Offerings at a Shinto Shrine. Courtesy of Martin Palmer/Circa Photo Library. **161** Worshippers at the Minatogawa Shrine, Kobe. Courtesy of Mary Evans Picture Library. **163** Shrine to Spirits of Dead Babies and Children. Courtesy of Martin Palmer/Circa Photo Library. **164** Ritual Dance of the Shinto Shrine Priests. Courtesy of AKG. **165** Guru Nanak. Courtesy of Twin Studio/Circa Photo Library. **167** 11 Gurus Guru Nanak in Centre. Courtesy of Bipinchandra J. Mistry/Circa Photo Library. **169** Reading the Guru Granth Sahib. Courtesy of John Smith/Circa Photo Library. **171** Golden Temple at Amritsar. Courtesy of Bipinchandra J. Mistry/Circa Photo Library. **172** Khalsa Sikh. Courtesy of Bipinchandra J. Mistry/Circa Photo Library. **173** Sikh Boys at Festival Procession. Courtesy of Twin Studio/Circa Photo Library. **174** Sikh Wedding. Courtesy of John Smith/Circa Photo Library. **176** Buddhist Statue at Luoyang, China. Courtesy of Tjalling Halbertsma/Circa Photo Library. **177** Kuan Yin, Northern Heng Shan Taoist Mountain. Courtesy of Tjalling Halbertsma/Circa Photo Library. **178–9** Hanging Temple. Courtesy of Tjalling Halbertsma/Circa Photo Library. **180** Taoist Priest. Courtesy of Tjalling Halberstma/Circa Photo Library. **182** Zoroastrian Fire Temple. Courtesy of Barnaby's Picture Library. **184** Fire Worship of Zoroastrians. Courtesy of Mary Evans Picture Library. **185** Zoroastrian Fire Temple of a Hillside Near Isfahan, Iran. Courtesy of Barnaby's Picture Library. **186** Towers of Silence. Courtesy of Barnaby's Picture Library. **188** Fire Worship. Courtesy of Barnaby's Picture Library. **188** Adoration of the Magi. Courtesy of AKG.

Index